THE PROPERTY GAME

TAG

Quantity discounts are available on bulk orders.
Contact sales@TAGPublishers.com for more information.

TAG Publishing, LLC
2618 S. Lipscomb
Amarillo, TX 79109
www.TAGPublishers.com

Office (806) 373-0114
Fax (806) 373-4004
info@TAGPublishers.com

ISBN: 978-1-934606-03-2

Cover: Lloyd Arbour, www.tablloyd.com
Text: Daniela A. Savone

First Edition

THE PROPERTY GAME

Winning in Real Estate

William Barnes

Contents

Foreword

Congratulations! By picking up this book, you've already won the property game.

Many of the world's richest individuals helped to significantly increase their financial worth by buying and investing in real estate. However, newcomers to the real-estate market, and even experienced real-estate investors, might find their minds bogged down with difficult questions, such as when is the right time to buy, is this the right property for me, and what should I be aiming for?

But real estate doesn't have to be a dredge of insecurities and questions. In fact, buying property can be fun, and as author Bill Barnes suggests in his book, it can be a game. Whether you prefer Monopoly or baseball, real estate can be a game that anyone can enjoy.

Barnes breaks down the rules of the game into nine simple chapters—his approach is almost so easy, it's scientific. This should be no surprise, considering Barnes made the leap to real estate from a science background. His book is well organized, easy to understand, and chock full of tips. For instance, Barnes tells you how to scout for a good deal. He also shows you how to conduct a practice before the big game, how to choose a team, and ultimately, how to hit a home run.

If you want to enter the real-estate market, there are a lot of books that you could buy. There's a lot of advice that you could seek. But none of them even come close to what you'll get out of The Property Game. If you don't see your business as a game, and you on a winning-streak, then you're missing out on all the fun.

—Gerry Robert, author of *Millionaire Mindset*

Introduction

Haven't You Always Wanted to Play Ball?

Baseball and capitalism. These two concepts are as American sounding as the crack of a bat against a ball and the roar of fans while the winning run is still in play. Children and adults love baseball—even though it often involves moments of apparent nothingness as athletes do their best to prevent the other team from advancing. But when the action occurs, it is momentous. We leave ball games with excited memories, even if our team lost. Home runs and exceptional outs remain vivid.

Baseball terminology has colored the English language and the business world. The phrase "home run" describes a hit in baseball as well as business deals and other personal efforts that pay off.

Real estate has been an indicator of wealth from time immemorial.

In today's lagging economy, we've all sat by and watched, feeling powerless as the stock market plummeted and people around the world found their investments suddenly worth half or less. Those who took advantage of special mortgage terms and spent more on housing because they qualified on paper found themselves in danger of losing their homes or seriously considering downsizing. Along with downsizing, many investors began looking at alternative investments. When these conditions occur, with falling prices and investors looking to unload properties, it is a perfect time to get into the game!

In winter 2008, you could drive around any upscale neighborhood and notice how many homes were for sale, while midlevel housing remained stable. Housing is an investment opportunity that, done correctly, can produce a stable income in an unstable environment.

I moved from New York to Arizona because of the cost of living and the climate. As a native New Yorker, I was a baseball fan, but I realized that my quality of life was better in Arizona. In fact, I even changed careers. My educational background is in science. As our world changes and we begin to look at the many fabulous areas in our country to live, raise families, and retire, it has become clear that I chose wisely. I love what I do, and I decided to write this book to help others achieve a similar winning feeling.

Winning big in real-estate investing conjures up different images for different people. We don't all want the same thing. We don't all aspire to play in the major leagues, but some of us do wish to play in the minor leagues or on the collegiate level. The common thread for all humans is a life of adequate or abundant income in order to reduce stress about money. Stability is a goal for everyone—though most of us wish to hit a home run that allows us to be millionaires or billionaires. Whether you are an investor who wishes to own just a few properties or you want to develop a huge property portfolio, this book is a great place to start. We all must continue learning. Laws change, as do markets and business strategies. With just a little effort, however, this game can be part of your personal financial plan—and it's not only enjoyable, it also aligns you with like-minded people.

Using the concepts presented in this book, you will build a team. If you've ever played ball, even Little League, you can probably still remember the friendships and associations of those days. Use that same enthusiasm now to re-create the fun on a new business level and enjoy the process.

No matter what your financial goals are, real-estate investing is a bonus to any financial portfolio. In the following chapters, I've presented the steps to creating a successful venture, including choosing your team members to help you select, improve, and maintain properties; finding deals or bargains; obtaining financing; and managing rental properties. This is indeed a noble, worthwhile, and profitable business in which we can provide quality housing and business space for the communities of our choosing. Knowing you can make money and provide a bare necessity of life, why not take your at-bat in real estate?

Are you ready to play? Real-estate investing is not only profitable—even in a struggling economy—it is also enjoyable. Any business venture should be done in a spirit of joy, just as sports are played by those with passion for the game. And the best part of investing in a struggling economy is that economic conditions will improve, meaning investment properties have even more potential to become home runs! To borrow a phrase from the 1951 Dodgers–Giants series, investing can be your "shot heard 'round the world."

Chapter One

Choosing Your Team and Picking Players

Part I: Scheduling Your Season

Throughout the ages, people who've held land have been considered the wealthiest. Why is that? It's because of human desire—and it has started wars, feuds, and competitions to hold land and property. When a peasant woman was accused of witchcraft in the Middle Ages, the first act after a guilty verdict was to seize all her property. It wasn't always about the crime committed but what holdings could be gleaned by removing the "criminal" from society. Scholarly studies suggest that accusations were often leveled against women who held land. They weren't "possessed," yet they did possess land, so they were seen as threats to others in less stable financial positions—often the nobility, whose debt-to-income ratio may have been compromised! Stealing real estate is not the topic of this book, though finding the best deals is a big issue. No one wants to overpay. And no one wants to suffer the hassles of land disputes. All of these ancient issues are still alive in the market today, but now our laws are more complex and favor you benefiting from your transactions.

Real estate as an investment is one of the oldest business transactions in history. It has always been seen as an indicator of financial stability, abundance, and prosperity. That you have this book in your hands indicates that you are interested in investing in real estate. Why people choose this real-estate investing varies from person to person, but often they are ready to move away from careers that are unfulfilling, boring, or no longer suited for them. I often find, too, that investors think this is something they can do on their own. Well, the truth is that yes, *you can* do better on your own—if you have a network of people whose specific jobs support you in your investing process. We do not have to face this process alone. In fact, it isn't even prudent. Whether you're a first time real-estate investor or a seasoned investor looking to expand your portfolio, I have some advice for moving forward in this exciting and lucrative market.

So where do we start? The first step should be goal setting. No team or athlete would begin a game without a game plan. They set goals and have a written strategy. The first part of this chapter is dedicated to goals (e.g., SMART goals) and writing a business plan or even a plan of action. The business plan does not have to be an elaborate document. However, it should contain your goals and the necessary steps to achieve them. To be successful at this business or any other business, one must first determine the objective. Set your goals. Begin to formulate near- and long-term goals. These can always be reexamined, and they should be updated as goals are met and exceeded, just as a team will reevaluate its strategies from inning to inning—and sometimes a time-out is necessary to see if your immediate goals will help you achieve your long-term goals. Any goals not reached in the intended time frame can always be revisited.

What do I mean by SMART goals? SMART is an acronym for goals that are **S**pecific, **M**easurable, **A**ttainable, **R**elevant, and **T**ime-based.

A **specific** goal is simple and easy to describe. When you set goals, are they specific and precise? "I want to be rich" is not specific. "I want to earn $1 million per year" is specific. Be clear and specific. Instead of setting a goal to own two rental properties, be specific about size, value, and location. Finding pictures to help you visualize can be motivating. A specific goal in real-estate investing would look something like "I own five rental properties valued at $200,000 each."

A **measurable** goal is one that has a specific outcome. How will you know when you've reached your goal? For example, the goal of saving $100,000 in a year is measurable. On December 31, you have either reached the goal or you haven't. It can be easily measured or documented.

An **attainable** goal is one that allows you to stretch, but it is not impossible. Let's say your goal is to make $1 million. If you are currently out of work and sitting home watching television and surfing the Internet, this goal is not very achievable. If financial prosperity is a goal, start by working and investing and then move on to the next attainable goal.

A **relevant** goal is one that has personal meaning for you and perhaps your family. It reflects who you are and what you value as a human being. It should be something that gives you joy. If you want to lose weight, connect that desire to a larger intention. Living a healthy and fit life is the larger intention that makes a weight-loss goal relevant. Choose things that make a difference in your life.

A **time-based** goal is one that has an end date. Even if you don't know if you can accomplish your goal in the time frame you've chosen, set a date anyway. Human minds respond to specifics.

One of the reasons goal setting has such a bad reputation is that we often confuse a goal with a task. If you don't experience a resounding yes as you create goals for yourself, then you are creating tasks. You are creating another variation of a to-do list. If you experience relief when a goal is achieved, you have set a task for yourself, not a goal.

What do you want? What is really important to you? Look at what you gravitate toward for fun. This is a great place to start making SMART goals. Remember, goals are part of the process that moves you toward your dreams.

It has been said that those who fail to plan, plan to fail, and this is very true when it comes to real estate. You need to know what type of property you want to acquire and what your exit strategy will be. So right now, take some time to write out a list of SMART goals. I've included a blank worksheet in the appendix, so you can **do it now**.

Part II: Choosing Your Team

After you decide on your game strategy, you need to decide who you need on your team. This type of investing is not to be taken lightly. However, continuing the analogy of an effective sports team, a few familiar ideas will help you understand the nature of the real-estate business. You *will need* players on your team for acquisition, financing, business, property management, and sales. You are the general manager (owner). As with all successful teams, you will need a coach and players. One need not play all positions to identify the best players. But you do need to be able to identify talent.

Your mission is to identify key members of your team and define their roles, and then determine criteria for selecting professionals to help you build and support a successful real-estate team.

It is important to remember that YOU are the most important member of your team. YOU are the leader, the general manager, and owner! You are the CEO of your business, and you are responsible for its success, even if you are just in the goal-setting and planning stages of this exciting venture. It is imperative to invest in licensed, professional services to help you stay informed about rules, regulations, and laws that could affect your business. Learn to leverage other people's knowledge, time, talent, and money. Build strong relationships with your team by practicing your people skills, which will foster loyalty in your team; this is critical. Get to know the various members personally and professionally. Develop close working relationships by operating with integrity, honesty, respect, and responsibility. But most important, be informed!

To qualify members of your team, interview each of them. An important question is "Are you an investor?" Other questions include "How long have you been in this business and investing?" and "How many and what types of properties do you have?" Consider asking, "Do you have real-estate investors as clients?" Continue with such inquiries as: "What licenses, designations, and credentials do you have? Who's your backup? When and how do you get paid, and what are your fees and/or commissions? How do you like to communicate (e.g., phone, email) and in what time frames? What services do you provide? What is your staff support structure? What types of deals can you bring? How often do you find deals? How big is your network?" As you build your team, you will learn to adjust these questions to suit your style and ambition.

Always ask for references, and ask open-ended questions that will allow them to educate you on what they are willing to do for you. As you go through the various members of the team, you will need to develop specific questions. I will provide suggestions in subsequent chapters and sections.

I can't emphasize enough that you will need a REALTOR® for both acquisition and selling. You will need to consider the following criteria for acquisitions: the market, state (location) and property type (raw or developed), carrying costs, holding times, rehabilitation costs, and new construction costs. You must also consider the amount of money needed and/or available, your financial position as well as that of the people with whom you will be partnering, your debt-to-income ratio and reserve funds, cash flow, etc. Each of your team members will be mentioned in more detail in subsequent chapters, but my intention here is to familiarize you with the job of each team member. Some of them will operate in a number of jobs, just like ball players can often play a number of positions.

A mentor or coach can assist in creating and implementing a business plan and help you reach your goals and objectives, both in business and on a personal level. A coach offers the highest degree of support and might be paid a high fee and work with you on a regular basis. An advisor might be your attorney, accountant, or financial planner. A mentor might be a friend or business partner who provides advice and council at no charge. If you decide to use a coach or mentor, make sure they understand your life and investment goals. Get a time commitment up front, and keep them updated about your progress and how their suggestions have worked. Look for motivators, leaders, and achievers—and investors.

As you begin investing in real estate, some of the first players used for acquisition will be "bird dogs," or scouts and REALTORS®. Their job is to scout out and find the best deals on the market and report to you in a timely manner. They are your line coaches and practice coaches; they are often experienced players. Timing is very important for finding some properties, such as preforeclosure properties or sherriff's auctions and those offered by the U.S. Marshals Service. Real estate agents (REALTORS®) and wholesaler partners will also be of assistance in this area.

Property managers are necessary when you're investing in states in which you do not reside or spend much time. It is rare than anyone can manage property effectively from afar, just as it is often difficult for the coach to handle the day-to-day business affairs of a professional team. That is the responsibility of a team manager who handles the outfitting and operations. If your property is located in another state, you will need a resident agent in that state to provide a local address for your entity.

Section 1031 exchange agents should be on your roster if you intend to buy and sell properties and defer taxes until a later date. Section 1031 of the IRS code lets you sell a property and buy a new property without paying any taxes (at the time of sale), but you must use an accommodator to comply with the rules. This is not an area most of us feel comfortable venturing into alone. The best pitcher in the world needs an excellent catcher. We might look at a 1031 exchange company/agent as a catcher. He or she can save the game. You are required to follow the law even if you don't know what the law is! The IRS is *very strict* when it comes to the time periods involved in a 1031 exchange. It is imperative that you choose a 1031 exchange company that has been in business for a long time and has agents who are educated, knowledgeable, and experienced. Questions for this position include: "How long you have been an agent? How do you get paid? How often and on what timetable do you like to communicate, and via which medium? What happens if I miss a deadline?" I'll discuss this more in Part III of this chapter and then again in chapter 8.

Appraisers, inspectors, and surveyors should be individuals who have good reputations and fair-market fees. These individuals or companies can make the difference between your investment being a sound purchase or a waste of money. These are your field positions, though you may find them moving up to cover the bases. Questions for these players include those regarding experience, knowledge of the area, and time frame in which they can usually get to a property. You may even, at first, choose those who come recommended by REALTORS® or other real-estate professionals.

Finally, licensed contractors with great, proven track records of quality and timely work will not only improve your investment but prevent you from being tied up in a lengthy, overextended project (both in time and money). These men and women cover your bases. As with other professionals, ask for references and ask to see some of their work. Also ask how long they have been in the business and what they consider their strengths or job preferences. Though this list may seem overwhelming, it gradually becomes easier to add to your team because you will develop business relationships, and your partners can make recommendations about other professionals as well as potential properties.

A motivated seller should also be considered a team member. Again, although they will probably not play in the next inning, like a pinch hitter, they can be great assets. It is a good idea to ask why a seller is motivated. You may find bargaining power. Is there a problem with the property, or do they wish to join their family? Is there a financial issue they are looking to escape? Such a motivation may have its perks.

Part III: Getting Sponsors

Financial- and business-team members are long-term players. When determining your real-estate strategy, such as fix and flip, buy and hold, foreclosures, short sales, multifamily, probate purchasing, or wholesaling, these professionals will help you determine and acquire the appropriate type of loan. In order to do this effectively and efficiently, you must keep good records. Maintaining financial statements, both business and personal, is a priority. Some novices think they will set this up once they make money. This is a big mistake because it is usually not a good idea to mix your personal and business monies, even at the beginning. Though financing options may require you to initially secure your loans with personal funds and income, you want to separate this. Maintaining separate financial statements from the beginning will make your accounting much easier and clearer. A bookkeeper and/or CPA should be chosen early in the recruiting process. They will play the entire game in a key position. You need them. They're always there. They're covering a lot of ground, so you may only see them monthly, but their position is crucial.

An accountant is another critical individual for your team. Your accountant will prepare and file your tax documents and financial statements. In general, a certified public accountant (CPA) is most qualified, followed by an accountant, and then a tax preparer. He or she should be familiar with setting up and working with multiple entities, 1031 exchanges, how to write off medical expenses, IRAs and profit sharing, be capable of creating profit-and-loss statements, and have access to or handle bookkeeping and payroll services. He or she should have access to legal and financial planning advice. Ask for fee schedules and find out how he or she gets paid. When working with an accountant, it is important to *maximize* your tax credits and *minimize* your taxable income. Ask your accountant how this will be done. Strategic calls and emails to your accountant should be free of charge to get simple questions answered. Your accountant should also be an investor. View your accountant as a team player who would be able to play several positions well and who is able to bat, pitch, and slide home. He or she is probably a good overall athlete.

Bookkeepers are not the same as accountants. They will track expenses, income, assets, and liabilities as part of your business at a substantially lower rate than a CPA. They should be able to do monthly, quarterly, and annual reports, which will be vital for not only your cash flow issues but also for financing options. Bookkeepers should be able to input data into your accounting program (e.g., QuickBooks), and they should be able to coordinate with the accountant and use similar or the same financial programs. Make sure you know how they get paid (e.g., hourly or monthly). Typically, bookkeepers do not provide tax services, however they can be financial planners. You can be your own bookkeeper if you have a good filing system and software program, but if you choose to pay someone to keep your books, be sure to ask specific questions regarding education, experience, other clients, and whether or not they are familiar with real-estate investing or are investors themselves.

TIP: Make sure your attorney, accountant, and bookkeeper do not nickel-and-dime you on fees and charges.

Obtaining a prepared list of standard fees for specific services should be part of your interview process.

As you get financially organized, one of the key steps is to form your corporate structure. Seek *legal and financial* assistance from a qualified professional to establish yourself as an LLC, partnership, or other formal business entity. Be sure to ask what other types of accounts they have and their area of specialty. Choose legal and financial team members who not only handle your type of investment business but those who enjoy working in real estate. Again, ask if they are investors themselves. They may have personal recommendations and experience that would not be available from noninvestors. I see attorneys as first basemen.

It is imperative to treat your investment business as a business. Even if you are working it part-time, honor it and your effort with the same level of detail and organization you would use in any other organization or any other team, sports or otherwise, on which you have been. Dedicate specific hours to accomplish certain tasks, just as you would practice schedules and games. These will all be part of your formal business plan. This is very, very important for protecting assets and income—and tax deferment.

Financial team members should include at the minimum mortgage brokers, loan officers, lenders—both conventional and hard money, banks, an escrow and title company accountant or CPA, a bookkeeper, an attorney, an IRA custodian, a financial planner, and the very important 1031 exchange facilitator. All of these are in addition to personal and professional advisors, mentors, and coaches. You likely already know some candidates in your social or familial circle, so you might consider asking them for recommendations. However, carefully consider business arrangements with friends and family. Business and friendship do not always mix well, but you may find some excellent referrals. It's not as difficult to start as it may seem. Network with other investors and get their referrals, too. Clients who refer other clients are always greatly appreciated.

Finance Options

A mortgage broker finds loans through a large network of lenders and works with loan officers. A good broker will have access to conventional and hard moneylenders, and they will find the best loan package for your circumstances. Get a list of all fees and loan details in writing, up front, making sure you're aware of all front-end, back-end, and hidden fees. Check their educational background, how long they have been in business, their references, and most important, their license status in the state(s) where they operate. Be very careful to guard against mortgage fraud—if it sounds too good to be true, it usually is. A good mortgage broker is part of your batting lineup. Where you put this player will be determined by where you stand in the game. In other words, what type of financing is needed for this project?

A loan officer works with lenders to find the best loan package for your situation. The loan officer *must* work with a licensed mortgage broker and pay him with points (typically 1 percent). Make sure the loan officer is honest and ethical and will not encourage you to make false claims on your application and supporting documentation because *that is mortgage fraud*. The loan officer should be one of the first up at-bat. Get a list of all fees and loan details in writing, up front, making sure you know all front-end, back-end, and hidden fees. Check their educational background, how long they have been in business, and verify their references. Ask them how long and what experience they have with investors versus other home buyers. Finding one who is also an investor is a plus.

Conventional lenders traditionally make long-term mortgages, short-term mortgages, and offer home equity lines of credit (HELOCs). Get a list of all fees and loan details, in writing, to ensure you are aware of all front-end, back-end, and hidden fees. Create a list of lenders and categorize them based on your various investment strategies.

Not all lenders will match all your investment needs. You will need the services of several different lenders. Avoid losing valuable time by approaching the wrong lender or too many lenders at once. Be selective about who you approach, depending on your specific needs. Research lenders before you start the application process, because they will, for example, pull your credit, which will then affect your FICO score.

Hard moneylenders who specialize in short-term unconventional loans are typically individuals who will loan money directly to you. They may combine several private lenders and present this as a single package. They do not look for FICO scores, but rather they look at the property's income/expense analysis, value, and the deal itself. They charge high interest rates, from 12 percent to 24 percent, and they are paid four to ten points up-front on the loan. Hard-money loans generally are bridge-type loans that seldom last longer than 36 months; typically, they are less than a year. Get a list of all fees and loan details, in writing, to ensure that you are aware of all front end, back end, and hidden fees. Building a trusting relationship with hard- money and private lenders will help you because they typically close very fast (only a couple of days in some cases), and they can help when that special deal comes along and you need to close fast. This is like pulling in a relief pitcher. You may not use him or her often, but they are there when you need them and can often save the game.

Banks provide long- and short-term loans, credit cards, lines of credit, and HELOCs. You should categorize banks according to how their services match your investment strategies. As always, get a list of all fees and loan details (including how long their quoted rates are good), in writing, to ensure that you are aware of all front end, back end, and hidden fees. It is wise to work with several banks because no single bank will likely meet your investment needs. This can be time consuming, but it's well worth it because you will gain access to lines of credit, which can come in handy when you need money down to open escrow or close a deal. Banks are an excellent source of quick cash.

Title and escrow companies' jobs are to hold earnest money, perform title searches on the subject properties, insure (underwrite) the title for the buyer and lender, prepare and create closing documentation, coordinate closing, and collect and distribute funds at closing. Certain states use attorneys instead of title or escrow companies. The choice of which entity to use is governed by state law. In some states, such as Arizona, the title company performs many functions, including: performing the title work, insuring the title, and performing the closing functions. Make sure you receive a preliminary settlement statement and preliminary commitment to insure the title within five business days after escrow is opened. Make sure you provide the lender with contact information, a mailing address, and homeowner's association (if one is present) as soon as possible after opening escrow. Hint: you should have all of these formulated and in writing prior to opening escrow. Ensure you get at least three business days to review the HUD-1 statement. Last, since underwriting the loan can slow up the process, make sure you allow yourself enough time when setting the closing date.

In real-estate investing, an attorney's task is to give legal advice, consultation, and representation. Attorneys facilitate the creation of various entities as you begin your investment business (C-Corps, S-Corps, and LLCs), and in some states the attorney will *write the contract and act as an escrow agent* at the closing. They can also prepare eviction notices and handle tenant eviction. As always, ask for fee schedules and how he or she gets paid. Strategic telephone calls and basic emails to your attorney should be free of charge, so be sure to ask about this. Also, you should be able to get simple questions answered at no charge once you are already their client, and as in the case with accountants, easy online access to forms and templates should be available. It is a good idea to choose an attorney who is also an investor. Keep close watch on their fees and miscellaneous charges as these can escalate quickly. It is possible to arrange for "one-time fee service" or "all-in-one" pricing of settlement costs, where the lender will offer a flat rate for a list of services such as application, origination, appraisal, underwriting and processing, points, pest or termite inspection, credit reports, lender's attorney, flood certification, title search and title insurance, tax services, and recording. Compare this to services offered separately. It can be a better deal financially, especially considering your time spent arranging it all separately.

A 1031 exchange agent is a qualified intermediary who holds monies for tax-deferred exchange. It is important to know that a 1031 exchange escrow account must be in place before you close on your property. You have 45 days after closing to identify a new property and a total of 180 days from closing to close on the new property.

If you miss these dates, you will have to cancel the exchange and pay the IRS the taxes due. You will more than likely have to pay the exchange agent as well. Make sure you understand the rates and services offered by these agents. A thorough interview will educate you on the process and provide you with the necessary comfort level. As with all other team members, ask questions such as how they get paid and what happens when terms are not met and deals fall through. References are a must. And as with everyone else on the team, ask if they, too, are investors. Much more on this process will be discussed in chapter 8. Attorneys and 1031 exchange agents should be in the middle of the batting lineup. With bases loaded and two outs, these legal aids can save your game. Remember to let them do the job you pay them for, and *do micromanage*!

Your IRA custodian is a member of your team who facilitates self-directed IRAs to buy properties, land, tax liens, notes, and other items. You should receive monthly, quarterly, and annual reports in printed and electronic versions. Make sure you have a private web portal to access your account so that you can check your account status and balances at any time. Also check to see how quickly the custodian will distribute funds. This is very important, especially in instances of quick closings.

Property Management and Upkeep

Property-management considerations should include, first and foremost, significant thought about whether you are going to do it yourself or hire a management company. Does your team need a business manager for the day-to-day operations of rental properties? There are several factors to consider in this arena: (1) Your time—is your time better spent locating and acquiring properties rather than managing them? And (2) Where is the property located? If you purchase properties in other cities or out of state, can you effectively manage them? Are you going to have active or passive involvement in your properties? How involved do you wish to be in the day-to-day management of the property? For the small fee of 5 percent to 10 percent of monthly rents plus expenses and lease fees, hiring a manager is very likely going to be money well spent and time saved. Ask what services they offer. Also ask what they offer above and beyond what other management firms offer. There may be perks! They want your business, so asking for their selling points can help you better choose the company that is the best suited for you.

Other good questions for property-management firms and individuals include: "How many properties are you managing? What companies do you use for repair and maintenance?" Also see at what point *you* can get out of a contract with them. Request a list of properties they manage, and check them out to see how well they are maintained. Ask how they select tenants and handle late payments and evictions. Also, if you can, ask to speak with tenants or previous tenants about how they are treated. A good property-management company keeps tenants happy, within reason, because tenants are the ultimate source of your cash flow. If the tenant cannot get the management company to respond to a repair issue, this is a red flag for the "middle management" of your property. The property manager position is one you will probably need to fill for daily management of rental property, but not all investors choose to hold rental properties.

Selling: Capitalizing on the Investment

The diligent investor will watch for market changes and signs of changing property values. If, perhaps, a new road is to be built near an existing holding, what are the potential effects on your investment? When considering the sale of a property, one must pose certain questions to her team (and it is always a good idea to continually recruit new players). These questions would include: "What is the projected effect of this development?" Changes that might affect your property include geographic changes, school redistricting, natural disasters, or anything else that could change property value, such as crime. You'll also want to ask about current market trends in mortgages, the rental housing market in the area, and the price of your property relative to similar properties.

For the REALTORS® on your team, you can ask for a fair-market analysis on the property. If you like what you are told, then you may want an appraisal done on the home.

Team Members: Function, Responsibility, and Importance

A mentor or coach can assist in creating and implementing a business plan and helping you reach your goals and objectives—sometimes on personal levels as well as in business. A coach offers the highest degree of support and is sometimes paid a high fee to work with you on a regular basis. An advisor is a professional like an attorney, accountant, or financial planner who provides advice and council for a fee. A mentor could be a friend or business partner who provides advice and council at no charge. If you decide to use a coach or mentor, make sure they understand your life and investment goals. Get a time commitment up front and keep them updated about your life and progress and how their suggestions have worked. Look for motivators, leaders, and achievers—and investors.

Now it's time to see how these individual players come together as a cohesive and championship-bound team. REALTORS® or real estate agents and real estate brokers are especially helpful in negotiating and writing contracts. A side note: Some states require that contracts be written by an attorney! Check with the laws of your state or the state in which the subject property is located. Realtors can guide you in this, as well as help you locate potential properties and market your property. They are excellent local resources for references to handymen, contractors, surveyors, engineers, architects, builders, inspectors, appraisers, title companies, and escrow officers. Remember, it is your responsibility. You *must* always check out the recommendations. It is definitely not too soon to familiarize yourself with the phrases "caveat emptor" and "due diligence." They mean "Let the buyer beware!" and "Do your homework!" respectively. The people with whom you work all provide a service for which you will pay. Be sure to check credentials and references for each one as you would any other type of employee.

Wholesalers buy properties below market value. They can be a source for properties such as foreclosures, auctions, and abandoned homes, which can sometimes provide higher returns. When dealing with wholesalers, always ask for incentives and promotions, and verify their comparables and rents. You will need to have your legal team review their contracts. Always do your due diligence on their deals, especially on distressed, foreclosed, or abandoned properties. Be prepared to close quickly. Like any other sale items, the best deals go to the person who is ready to buy.

A partner is someone who can provide experience, time, and money and who will share your profits and losses. You may not need to use a partner, or you may choose to have a partner on some deals to spread risk. Partners can be people you know from business, friends, or family members, but remember that much of your personal information, such as FICO scores and financial statements, will be shared among partners. Most important when dealing with a partner is to *put all agreements in writing and include terms and conditions. Have an attorney review all contracts, define responsibilities carefully, and then monitor this responsibility. Be sure to create a legal entity for liability and asset protection.*

The function of a resident agent is to provide you with a permanent address in a state in which you do not reside so that you can conduct business there. Resident-agent fees vary from state to state and run $50 to $150 annually. Even if you use a web-based service, it is important to be able to reach this person on the phone. Get references, recommendations, and ask questions. And follow through with these references. Check them out!

An appraiser's job is to determine the value of properties; he or she also highlights property conditions and can sometimes provide you with an avenue of escape should you want to get out of a deal. An appraiser is held to legal and ethical standards, so you definitely want one to be fair to you without breaking the law. Again, appraisers play in both the top and bottom of all innings. They are on your side in all types of transactions.

Like appraisers, inspectors and surveyors are also very important because it is their job to thoroughly inspect the properties and survey land for easements and encroachments, as well as structures. Some inspectors can handle the entire property while others specialize in select areas such as roof, structural, basement, electrical, plumbing, et cetera. Home (building) inspectors can inspect the general condition of a property very early in the offer process and prior to the appraisal. *Never buy a property without first doing inspections.* As with the appraiser, sometimes inspectors can provide an avenue of escape. Lastly, hire only licensed and bonded inspectors. Like appraisers, they are held to legal and ethical standards. Know their track records and check for red flags.

Since general contractors handle major repairs or capital improvements, you are often investing large amounts of money with these professionals. Do not pay for labor until the job is completed. If up-front payment is required, pay the contractor a portion up front and the balance upon completion. Read all contracts and have them reviewed by a legal staff. If a certificate of occupancy is required by the local governmental agency, make sure you receive it prior to making the final payment.

Last in this seemingly never-ending list is the insurance agent. This is someone with whom you probably already work, but if your current agent does not meet the following criteria, you can seek his or her advice in finding the right agent. Specific to real estate investing, an insurance agent will provide you with landlord insurance for liability, flood, hurricane, tornado, and earthquake, or whatever is necessary. Insurance agents can provide umbrella insurance for properties covered by another insurance company. Also ask if they can provide loss-of-rent insurance. Make sure you require tenants to get renter's insurance to cover their belongings and liability as part of the lease. Have them provide proof of this if that's allowed.

Though this recruiting process may seem daunting, once you choose your first team members, the rest will come via recommendations and contacts. They *want* your business. They want you to succeed. Take the time to choose your team wisely and always be willing to recruit players who impress you.

Chapter Two

Scouting for a Good Deal

The most common question from novice real-estate investors is, "So what makes a potential purchase a good deal?" There are a few common denominators that investors look for. However, if you are only looking at the seller's full retail price, or in some cases above retail price, and you are only thinking of using typical bank financing, then finding the good deals will be an *almost* impossible task.

A good deal is one that provides an opportunity for profit. Investors who look only at equity in a property are passing up many opportunities. Although buying property below fair-market value is the number one characteristic of a good deal, it is not the only one.

On a fundamental level, your might consider why you're looking to invest or find good deals. Sure, we all want to make money, but is that your only reason? Consider the advice of author and investor

Dan Auito, whose article "Finding Good Deals in Real Estate" posted to the Website www.ezinearticles.com, suggests that:

"A thriving real estate investor or retailer solves a lot of other people's problems; that's how you become successful. The more knowledge, ability, experience, contacts, and resources you have, the more solutions you can begin to offer people in solving their problems. In addition to this, you will be ahead of the pack if you can get people calling or coming to you with their specific problem first."

Auito suggests that in order to be really good at this game you must have your intentions prioritised. Are you investing simply to make money, or can you see how this business can also help other people, often in a time of crisis? When financial crisis looms for an individual or family, often their property falls into a state of physical decline. Then they feel the need to be bailed out. By seeing yourself as a problem solver, you'll build the skills to help others while building your own financial and real-estate portfolio.

Auito continues, "Advertise the fact that you are in a position to help while being fair, trustworthy, and accurate in making quick decisions before the competition tries to persuade these people first." This is how you'll find good deals and develop a reputation as an honorable business investor. It's tantamount to a recruiter selling the value of joining his team. What's the benefit of selling to you? What's the benefit of playing for this particular team? The deals will eventually come to you. But before that occurs, you need to get the word out by advertising or marketing your services as a problem solver.

Because real estate investing is competitive, you will need to understand marketing. That means deciding on what you are going to specialize in, developing a method to define your target audience, and then attracting them with a well-written message using different types of media.

What exactly do you want to specialize in? Following are some categories from which to choose:

- Condos and vacation property
- Single-family homes
- Apartments for one to four families (residential duplex, triplex, fourplex)
- Commercial: hotels/motels, strip malls, office complexes, mobile home parks, storage units, parking lots, garages, restaurants, stores, apartments for five or more families, etc.
- Industrial: factories, manufacturing plants, warehousing, etc.
- Farms: commercial, industrial, or agricultural, depending on zoning
- Raw land: lots, vacation and recreation, subdividable residential, commercial, industrial, agricultural, and special purpose

- Special purpose: churches, schools, hospitals, power plants, theatres, sports arenas, golf courses, marinas, etc.

Many real estate investors target properties that are distressed, vacant, or owned by motivated sellers. The objective is to create a deal and produce a profit. It could provide cash flow as a rental, it may be in an area where above average appreciation is expected, or both. A deal can be a property that is bought below market value and then immediately sold for a profit. Or it may require minor aesthetic changes to improve its value and appeal. This is known as "flipping." It may also be a property that is contracted and then assigned to another investor for a fee. Investors can even profit on properties that are purchased at fair-market value. By using alternative financing, investors can create streams of income. A deal can come in all shapes and sizes, but a good deal is a property where money can be made.

This process requires patience and diligence. Like any baseball game, one can only truly enjoy the game when fully giving one's attention to the action. Sometimes games seem to move along slowly, but when action does happen, when the crack of the bat sounds, you'll miss the play if you aren't paying attention. Play close attention to the real estate market in your desired areas: commercial, single-family, or multiunit. Be alert! And when the batter connects, follow the ball to see where it is going. With this type of mental alertness, you can be assured of finding the deals you are looking for.

The first and most important rule to remember is this: 10 percent profit, 10 percent holding costs, and 12 percent in repairs. This means you need to purchase the property 32 percent below the fair-market value. Based on this rule, you need to value each property, determined by the comparables, and assess whether or not it meets your criteria:

- A property that can be purchased below fair-market value
- A property that may produce positive cash flow through rental income or a lease/option
- A property that is expected to dramatically appreciate in value
- A property that offers favorable financing through the seller or a "subject to existing financing" deal

Properties that can be purchased at least 32 percent below market value are often targeted for fix-and-flip deals, options, assignments, finder's fees, lease options, and income properties. A maximum offer worksheet, which can be found in the Property Evaluation appendix, should be completed for every deal. This will help you calculate costs and determine how much to offer the seller. You may need to enlist other team members to help as estimates, fees, and other variables may fluctuate based on the condition or location of the property.

Positive cash flow can be created from income properties, lease options, agreement for deeds, and investor-held loans. Cash flow is the movement of money in and out of your business over a defined period of time (weekly, monthly, or quarterly). If cash coming into your business exceeds the cash going out of your business, your company has a positive cash flow. However, if your cash outflow exceeds the cash inflow, then your company has a negative cash flow. To create a positive cash flow, generate more cash and collect the cash in a timelier manner while maintaining or reducing your expenses. There are a number of ways to do this in real estate investing. An investor may pay full price for a property if the income it produces covers all of the expenses involved and there is money left over.

Most investors will not buy properties solely based on expected appreciation because of the uncertainty of the future. However, there are those who follow the market closely and who can recognize market trends, development opportunities, and potential zoning changes. Again, the growth rate of an area can be researched, and the local government may be able to provide a ten-year plan for the area's development. Properties can be held as income properties in these areas, or investors can use pure options to speculate. Pure options defer tax liability and do not require management because they do not come with tenants. They can be exchanged, used as down payments, used in a buy/sell strategy, used to control assets without ownership, or used as payment in lieu of installments due.

Favorable financing that requires no down payment and can be had at a good interest rate, or that is nonqualifying, can allow investors to leverage a large amount of real estate. Assuming any loan by purchasing a property "subject to existing financing" is a favorite among seasoned investors. Even a property purchased at market value can provide a money-making opportunity if the financing is right. Financing can often be the deciding factor when considering an investment property, so again, pulling in other team members to compare financing options, the terms of the existing financing agreement, and legal clauses or stipulations of the contract is crucial until you learn to identify these issues on your own.

Analyze each property to see which investment strategies may apply. Try to satisfy the seller's needs by considering all the possible solutions available. It is important to learn all the investment strategies to ensure that a potential deal doesn't pass by unnoticed, including:

1. Target your properties—buy a property you understand.
2. Evaluate your strategy.
3. Visit and inspect the property.
4. Choose your investment property and have a plan for the property.
5. Calculate your profit (research and evaluate).
6. Submit your offer.
7. Negotiate the contract (use positive leverage).
8. Reinspect with a professional inspector—renegotiate if necessary.

9. Close on the property.

10. Repair, rent, and/or sell.

Locating the properties themselves requires time and effort, but you can make this easier by working with bird dogs, realtors, or even enlisting the help of family members. Here are some examples of how you might go about finding some good deal on your own: Check out bulletin boards, local papers, independent publications, and the Internet. Each city, town, and village has its own favorites. See where the locals go to get their good deals. This goes for every publication. Make sure you get one of the first copies off the press. Go to the press office and get your copy before the ink has a chance to dry.

Advertise yourself in the same publications so that people who are thinking about selling will call you before they tell the world through an ad or list with a REALTOR®. Make it a habit to look at the legal section of the newspapers. Contact heirs and attorneys, and visit estate and moving sales. Also, 20 percent of people who have garage sales are planning on moving soon. Ask about their house or their neighbors' homes. Always keep your antenna up!

Your odds of success increase when you choose large population centers and remain in the market, constantly on the lookout for your type of deal. When we put effort into looking for what we want, we tend to find it. Use the Law of Attraction to focus on what you want versus what you don't want in order to draw things to you. Think of the deal in the neighborhood or town you want and begin to take notice when you even get close to these properties.

Look for vacant houses that are run down, fire damaged, or abandoned. Look for city notices. Talk to the neighbors. They usually know who owns it and what is going on. They have an interest in seeing it restored to maintain the neighborhood integrity. Walk up to a property and look in a window to confirm that it is indeed vacant—but don't endanger yourself! Use common sense. Contact out-of-state owners through property records or by letter and/or phone. Leave your cards on the door. Get creative in your approach to finding properties.

REO or OREO stands for Real Estate Owned and Other Real Estate Owned. This is how lender-owned properties are referred to. These types of properties have been taken back by the lender due to foreclosure and can often be had for a fraction of the actual value. Make friends with your local lenders and let them know you are the one to call when they have a foreclosure looming or in progress.

Considering the massive meltdown in the real-estate market and the thousands on thousands of foreclosures nationwide, it's easy to find distressed or foreclosed properties at rock-bottom prices. The issue now is financing, but if you have cash on hand, or even have retained good credit, fantastic investment opportunities are everywhere. There is also ample opportunity to help others get out of properties in which they were simply in over their heads from choosing to take advantage of some bad financing choices such as interest-only loans and income to debt ratio changes in their lives.

Hint: if you prequalify with lenders beforehand, they may call you sooner.

Use www.foreclosure.com and watch the local paper for foreclosure auctions, tax sales, and HUD- and Veterans Affairs–listed properties. Auctions held in bad weather where the property absolutely must be sold are your best chance to limit competition and get property at rock-bottom prices. Because there is no low limit on what can be accepted (no reserve), you may win big.

Good real estate agents want to help you find what you're looking for. They want to help you buy because that's the only way they get paid. When you approach them, be very specific and tell them to call only if they have an absolute steal. Ask agents to give you expired listings they couldn't sell. Suggest a 2 percent commission if they assist with closing the paperwork after you make a deal with the seller on your own.

Don't be too selective. If the property is an absolute steal, lock it up and sell it to somebody who likes to work with that type of real estate. Get an option and hand it off to another buyer. Look for distressed sellers in addition to distressed property.

Post fliers everywhere—colleges, laundromats, shopping centers, bowling alleys, public bulletin boards, churches, local businesses—wherever large numbers of people congregate. Give people a chance to give you a lead. For example, print cards that say, "I pay you $500 at closing if I buy a house you told me about! Do you know anyone who is selling property? Please call [your name] at 555-1212." Print quality business cards, as this small detail shows your level of professionalism.

Join organizations of all types. The sky is the limit. There are so many—just pick the ones you are interested in and let it be known you pay bounties for consummated (closed) deals.

When you use bird dogs, leave out no one. Property managers, moving companies, relocation services, neighbors, landlords, tenants, the mailman, the paper boy, gardeners, landscapers, service technicians, pest control people, friends, acquaintances, relatives, and other investors can all help. Consider enlisting the help of retired people who have time to scout neighborhoods and often visit estate sales. Older people are very valuable informants. They often know a lot about the area, and they also need people to talk to! Listen to them. Go to free seminars on real estate. Do this not only to learn about real estate but also to capture names and circulate among real-estate-minded people. Once you have their names, call your own club meeting and network. The most important thing is to *put yourself out there*!

Everyone should know they can make $500 or whatever amount if you end up buying a property they tell you about. Enlist your army!

Give each of your soldiers a stack of your cards. Water, gas, and electric company personnel, who shut off utility meters, can be very good bird dogs when it comes to finding property that is in trouble or vacant, as can cable and satellite television installers, who may notice vacant homes on their routes. Make sure they have your cards! Have at least 10,000 business cards printed with your offer and hand them out to everyone you can.

As you grow your business, you might consider TV, radio, phone books, billboards, street benches, bumper stickers, and bigger commissions for your bird dogs. Use your imagination. Brainstorm with partners and get advice from the successful investors in your circle. Networking organizations are a good idea because they will put you in the circle of people who are also investing and whose businesses may support yours and vice versa.

Talk to sellers and find out why they want to sell. Knowing the seller's motivation to sell will help you in negotiations. Try offering 15 percent less than what you intend on paying. You never know; the seller may accept, depending on their motivation and urgency. If they don't, you can still negotiate up to 15 percent more and get it for what you originally were willing to pay. If it's any higher, walk away, but leave the offer on the table (the offer stands). Make your offer easy for the seller to understand. Get the option to buy but use a contingency to protect yourself. Iron out the details later, but lock it up now!

Initially, it's a good idea to buy from sellers who tend not to care: seized, foreclosed, tax sales, corporations, nonprofits, disinterested heirs, probate attorneys, and private auctions. Try helping someone sell his or her property even if you don't want it. Be a friend and offer to help for nothing in return. You will be amazed at what happens when you sincerely try to help with no thought of making money. This is a magic bullet in disguise.

The old saying in real estate is "You make your profit when you buy, not when you sell." There is no good or bad time for investing in the real-estate market. There are plenty of opportunities to make money at all times. The best thing is there are so many different ways you can approach this type of investing. Find those ways you feel comfortable with and make the most of the resources and people who come your way. It's important to *treat it as a business* and don't let emotions get in the way of a good deal. Find a balance between helping people and making money for yourself, and you'll be a success. Creating a win/win situation will make you a success in the long term. Remember, real-estate investing is a long-term game. You do not win a game in the first inning; it takes nine innings to complete the game.

Chapter Three

Practice before the Game

Finding the right property is like practicing for a game or rehearsing for a performance. You cannot choose randomly, just as an athlete cannot effectively participate in any sport without first practicing his position and interacting with his team. When you begin looking for property, you will need to interact with your team members to see how you can count on them and in what capacity. If your specialists have limited schedules, you need to know when to contact them. Also, one may not, for example, want to invest in certain properties when the liabilities are too great. The ability to know what to look for will develop as you continue to search, evaluate, and work the figures on each one.

Don't be afraid to recruit new members when existing players fail to play well. Not all personalities fit in every situation. It does not need to be a personal or lifetime commitment with your team members. You may find that as you go along, some professionals do well in some arenas and not in others. Also, you will want to look for those whose personalities and professional expertise fit with your goals and your schedule. It does you no good to have the top-producing mortgage broker or realtor if you can never contact them or get them when *you* need them.

All areas of business require that an effective team be in place. Sometimes this requires the termination of a business arrangement in order to bring on new or more effective players. This is true in sports, real estate, or any other business arrangement. It is easy to see the necessity for this when we compare our business practices to professional ball teams. Their work is on display for public consumption. Be sure to look within and get guidance. Use your mentor.

If we compare the rashness of the sports world to slashing and burning our staff, we might learn to first look at our own actions, evaluate the team, see what talent we have on board, and then make adjustments. Some of the biggest sports news is often about the current status of team management and coaching staff. Often the news is most on the minds of the fans that are not privy to all of the details, whether contractual or personal. Be careful when including friends and family on your team because if things go wrong and you find yourself needing or wanting to change your lineup, your fans may become critical too.

This sports comparison can help us to form our teams well, know the competition, and recognize what we're up against. Who is bidding against you? Who are the team members? How do they operate? Are they knowledgeable and fair players, or are they known for last minute or underhanded operations? I always suggest being an ethical investor, but know your opposition and how they're likely to play against you. Even a bad season can be turned around. Mediocre teams can have good games. Great teams can play poorly. Each investment can be seen as a new game

Often a new coach, manager, or even players can help you turn your season or game around by bringing fresh ideas and attitudes into even a single game. But as in sports, sometimes team members are short-term solutions. In real estate, with each investment property compared to a single game, it might produce a winning solution for the entire season. For long-term success, however, it is typical for the team to have been together for a while. As with all sports and business arrangements, a winning streak may occur temporarily, though you may still consider scouting for other talent.

Managing and coaching professional and semiprofessional sports teams is often a temporary job with a huge salary. Beware of treating your team members like temporary coaches with high salaries, but also understand that when you form a team, you must have people who are playing to win and who know their jobs. Otherwise, they may find themselves suddenly canned. It is *your* team. Treat it as such.

Each investment or purchase of real estate requires teamwork. But we can't just hope she shows up when we or our team members are in the right place at the right time. Doing your homework and paying attention to the smallest of details help pave the way for hitting home runs and making it to the playoffs.

There is a lot to be learned, especially in the practice of forming your team, including patience and the willingness to accept responsibility for one's own actions and the choices of players or support personnel. Remember that you are working with human beings, and errors, strikes, and foul balls will occur. But there does come a time for recruiting, replacing, and firing the staff and players. Be willing to learn, and always operate with integrity and honesty. Always protect your investments.

Firing Professionals

It is just a fact of life that some relationships, whether personal or professional, will either fail or evolve. If a relationship is not growing and changing, it is dying, so there are going to be times to sever or change these arrangements in order to protect or grow your business. Firing anyone is not usually a pleasant task, and this is even more difficult when the team member is a legal professional.

In some business arrangements, we often forget that we, too, are clients, and we have the right to choose another. With legal services, however, there is usually a contract involved, and these things can get very sticky. Before sending your attorney to the locker room and asking him to return his or her uniform, consider what agreements you have in process and what the possible ramifications may be for removing this player.

Carefully consider your reasons for wanting to fire anyone. Is it a personal issue, a personality issue, or a bad decision on their part? Be sure your motives are based on sound business decisions. If your attorney's area of specialty does not meet your specific needs, this is a good reason to seek another more qualified one. If you feel your lawyer is not giving your case or situation adequate time and attention, this, too, is a good reason to find a new one. But if you simply did not like a ruling or judgment, this is not a reason to change lawyers.

Sometimes changing lawyers will be detrimental to your intended outcome, but if you feel compelled to change your legal representation, first communicate with him or her about your dissatisfaction. Communicate which areas cause you specific concern and attempt a resolution. Explain why you are considering seeking new representation and what would have to occur for you to remain a client. Since lawyers should want to keep clients happy, there may be a solution possible through negotiation.

There are many things to consider when firing an attorney, and the first is to carefully read your contracts or agreements you have with him or her. It may tell you what steps are necessary to cancel the arrangement. You should have your new attorney review the agreement before agreeing to take you on as a client, and he or she must be willing to help you move through the process as well. This will mean hiring a new lawyer before firing the existing one, which may tie up some funds, but this will expedite the transition from one to the other because you will want to have all information transferred. Will your new lawyer do this for you or is this your responsibility?

Also, some information will need to be communicated to the court system should you be in the middle of a legal proceeding.

All communication with the attorney leaving the team should be done in writing and via certified mail and copies sent to your new attorney if he or she is not handling the transition for you. Clearly state in your letter that the relationship is terminating and that all work on your case is to stop immediately. You need not go into detail about why you chose to fire him or her because much of that should have already been communicated when informing him or her about your dissatisfaction and should no longer be relevant.

You may be able to ask for a return of retainer fees or other monies paid up front, but consult your new attorney on this issue. He or she will likely want to see an itemized list of services provided to date to determine this. You'll also want a copy of this for your own records should any dispute occur in the future.

Firing your attorney can be frightening, but it is crucial to remain professional and leave your emotions out of the situation. It is not a personal issue, therefore it is imperative that you keep all communications cool, professional, and focused on the business issues. This will help to make it a smooth transition.

Equally as difficult as firing an attorney is firing a real-estate agent or any other players on your team. Most investors think that when they sign a contract with a realtor they are bound to it. We've all heard stories of realtors accepting a listing, posting it on the multiple listing service (MLS) without taking any action to market the property, and hoping it will just magically sell quickly. Considering the state of the market today, this is unlikely unless the property is listed well under fair-market value.

Remember, it's your property; they're your investments, and you deserve your realtor's best effort. *Before you sign anything, make sure you can cancel the contract under a nonperformance clause.* A house or any other real estate is a large investment that should be taken seriously. Your realtor should work with you in any and every capacity in which he or she agrees. If this agreement is not kept, then consider terminating the agreement and finding another.

As with legal representation, there is proper protocol to follow before just slashing a professional off your team. Again, is there a personal issue or is it really a case of a business arrangement that is not working out? Does your contract have legal issues that need to be resolved as well? Be sure your legal representation is in order before cancelling a contract with your realtor.

If you have a contract, be sure you understand it. If you have properties listed through this agent, you probably do have one. Often these contracts state a specified period; an end date may be listed along with services offered and the commission paid to the agent upon selling or obtaining a property for you. Some contracts have a clause enabling either party to break the agreement, but sometimes a commission is still expected to be paid. Some contracts will state that it may *not* be broken until the time has elapsed. Read the fine print. You and your realtor should have discussed which marketing strategies he or she intended to use. Was this done? Was it marketed properly and is still not selling, or was it underrepresented according to the agreement?

I suggest you only enter into contracts with a cancellation clause that allows dissolution of the relationship for nonperformance. We all have life situations that come up, and though you may be sympathetic to the reasons for the realtor not marketing your property, for example, it is to remain a business relationship and not a personal one.

If you do decide to cancel a listing or sever the relationship totally, first ask your realtor to cancel the listing. If he or she refuses, go to the broker and ask that it be cancelled there. Involving attorneys too quickly to do these will cost hefty legal fees. Also, should there be future involvement with the agent or broker, it is a good idea to keep your reputation clean and professional. Should both the agent and broker refuse, you have the right to contact the board of realtors for your state. Only once these options have been exhausted will you notify all parties of your intent to involve your real-estate attorney. Often this will be enough to release the listing, but if it is not, follow through and turn the situation over to that team member whose job it is to do so.

Cancelling Buyers' Agreements

Freeing yourself from a buyer's agreement, both written and oral, can be done with a form called a Termination of Buyer's Agency, available through your agent or real estate lawyer. As an investor, you may be asked by some agents to sign a Buyers' Agency Agreement. These are intended to protect both you and the agent. The agent agrees to deal with you honestly and with due diligence, and you agree to not cut the realtor out of the deal at closing. More and more people are trying to sell properties "by owner," and this is often an attempt to keep real estate professionals' fees out of the process. But if a realtor finds a property listed by the owner, and you purchase it, you will find yourself still owing fees. Failing to keep your end of a buyer's agreement may find you sitting alone on the diamond with no team members showing up for the game! Everyone is in business to make money. Shortchanging a realtor is no way to retain team members or get good service. You are expecting to make money off your real-estate investments. You cannot expect someone else to provide services for you at no cost.

Most conflicts can be handled with good communication. There are times when the cancelling of the agreements are in the best interest of both parties, so if you are unhappy with your agent, tell him or her why, attempt to reach an agreement, and if one cannot be reached, ask to be released for valid reasons. Finding a better deal through a different agent or a "by owner" deal is not worth the risk ethically or legally. Don't sneak into the game, and only wear the uniform if you are on the team. Do your homework and choose your players and realtor carefully to avoid having to fire (trade) a player. However, if you feel you need to, then "Just Do It!"

Chapter Four

Outfitting Your Team: Finding Financing Options

What does your financial situation look like? What type of uniform do you sport for financial backers? Knowing what you qualify for does not mean you should invest that much—but before you can be taken seriously in any negotiation, you have to know what you're qualified for. In this chapter, I give specific instructions to help you determine what price ranges and property types you can consider, using industry-specific formulas. I also include warnings for financial pitfalls such as zero-down financing.

In addition to explaining how to determine your financial qualifications, I will also discuss the different types of financing and financing institutions and help you choose those most appropriate for your given situation. There may be something hidden behind that low-interest rate and meager- or no-down-payment requirement. A number of these programs contributed to the 2008 mortgage crisis.

When one has "no skin in the game," there are too many opportunities to walk away. Investments are just that: skin in the game. Your time, energy, money, or skills will eventually pay off. There is an old adage that says "If it seems too good to be true, it probably is." Bear in mind this is true in the world of real-estate investment.

Though I'm not a fan of zero-down financing, what is presented to us in many forms of news is simply a worst-case scenario. Sensationalism sells. It is crucial to work with professionals in mortgage lending because it is their job to be up to date with the truth about the mortgage-loan industry, and not the hype presented by the media who aim to sell news stories and periodicals. Do your homework. Due diligence does not apply simply to investigating the property itself but also to remaining abreast of all the changes and fluctuations in the industry.

In my opinion, the issues were being blown out of proportion. Are the issues and practices that brought the United States to this point a problem? *Yes,* and they need to be addressed. Wall Street and Main Street America are having problems, and taxpayers are paying for it. We do need to make changes in the financial and mortgage industries. Perhaps it will require a complete overhaul. But in October 1987, the United States experienced Black Monday; in 1991, the United States had the savings and loan crisis. Real estate experienced dramatic losses in both instances. But it came back. In my opinion, over the long period, real-estate investing done properly will make profits.

Zero down requires no skin in the game. In addition to causing unsuspecting individuals and families financial damage, the investor market drove up the cost of homes by flipping houses using zero down. I know of a neighborhood in Arizona that is hurting because of the practice of flipping new homes by investors who were taking money out. For example, a home sells for $200,000, but due to inflated appraisals, is appraised at $225,000 and a mortgage is secured for that amount. So $25,000 goes into the pocket of the investor who has nothing invested, and then sells immediately at a profit. It is a bad thing ethically. Taking loans for 125 percent of the value of the property immediately puts you upside down in the house, unless you are lucky enough to sell quickly.

Overall, the economy is suffering because of these practices. If the bank didn't know it was a loan for 125 percent versus 100 percent, it is bank fraud. And if the appraiser appraised the house knowing that, then the appraiser is also liable. In my opinion, these acts of greed contributed to the housing crisis of 2008.

There is a lot of fraud in the industry, and this is a big reason for it. If you include the closing costs in the loan package, you have no skin in the game. What happens when economic players knowingly drive up costs even though the value isn't keeping up? The average home buyer or even the average investor will not be able to afford to buy in their desired neighborhoods.

Looking for the Best Mortgage

Shopping around for a home loan or mortgage will help you get the best financing deal. A mortgage—whether it's a home purchase, a refinancing, or a home equity loan—is a product just like a car, a piece of furniture, a boat, or a recreational vehicle, so the price and terms are often negotiable! You will want to compare all the costs involved in obtaining a mortgage (or any other type of loan). Shopping, comparing, and negotiating may save you thousands of dollars.

Obtain information from several lenders. They want your business. They'll also want to know what other lenders you're considering.

Obtain all-important information regarding the total cost of the loan. There may be costs about which you are unaware. Ask questions. Ask for a bottom line. Ask, "What are all the costs involved?" Get an itemized list in writing to make a line-by-line comparison easier.

Obtain the best deal you can. This may seem like an absurd statement, but some people will want to give their business to their brother-in-law's cousin, who just got started in the business. Though this young mortgage lender may indeed need the business, what is in *your* best interest? Remember to shop, compare, and negotiate. Your friend's brother-in-law's cousin may indeed work out for you, but only consider this person if the figures and terms are in your best interest!

Fair lending is required by law. This seems as common sense as fair housing laws or equal education rights, but beware, discrimination on a variety of issues still exists. If you feel you are being discriminated against for any reason, investigate it. Again, *use* your attorney. Fair lending is not limited to discriminatory issues. Issues such as excessive interest rates, points, et cetera. may be included. Know your rights.

Credit problems? There are a variety of loans for a variety of credit scores. First know yours. You need to know the scores from all three reporting agencies, but your FICO score is most important. When you see your credit report, be sure that all the information reported there is accurate. Is there something listed that is not yours? Contest it. Does it belong to your father with the same name? Have it removed. It may require some effort and proof of incorrect reporting, but it can make a huge difference in your ability to obtain a loan at a lower rate.

Obtain information from several lenders up front and in writing! Mortgage loans are available from several types of lenders: thrift institutions, commercial banks, mortgage companies, and credit unions. Different lenders may quote different prices, so you should contact several to ensure you're getting the best price. You can also get a home loan through a mortgage broker. Brokers arrange transactions rather than lending money directly; in other words, they find a lender for you, and they make money on the deal. A broker's access to several lenders can mean a wider selection of loan products and terms. Brokers will generally contact several lenders regarding your application, but they are not obligated to find the best deal for you unless they have contracted with you to act as your agent. They may have their own best interest in mind. Remember, everyone is in business to make money. Consequently, you should consider contacting more than one broker, just as you should with banks or thrift institutions.

Whether you are dealing with a lender or a broker may not always be clear. Some financial institutions operate as both lenders and brokers. And most brokers' advertisements do not use the word "broker." Ask if a broker is involved. This information is important because brokers are usually paid a fee for their services that may be separate from and in addition to the lender's origination or other fees. A broker's compensation may be in the form of points paid at closing or as an add-on to your interest rate, or both. You should ask each broker how he or she will be compensated so that you can compare the different fees. Be prepared to negotiate with the brokers as well as the lenders.

Obtain all important cost information in writing. Be sure to get information about mortgages from several lenders or brokers. Know how much of a down payment you can afford, keeping in mind that you do not want to put all of your cash down, and find out all the costs involved in the loan. You will need cash for moving costs, improvements if necessary, and possibly furniture or fixtures for your new home or investment. Knowing just the monthly payment or the interest rate is not enough. Ask for information about the same loan amount, loan term, and type of loan so that you can compare the information. The following information is important to get from each lender and broker.

Rates

Ask each lender and broker for a list of their current mortgage interest rates and whether the rates being quoted are the lowest for that day or week.

Ask whether the rate is fixed or adjustable. Keep in mind that when interest rates for adjustable-rate loans go up, generally so does the monthly payment.

If the rate quoted is for an adjustable-rate loan, ask how your rate and loan payment will vary, including whether your loan payment will be reduced when rates go down.

Ask about the loan's annual percentage rate (APR). The APR takes into account not only the interest rate but also points, broker fees, and certain other credit charges that you may be required to pay, expressed as a yearly rate.

Points are fees paid to the lender or broker for the loan and are often linked to the interest rate; usually the more points you pay, the lower the rate. Some loans, such as VA loans, have no points attached. Points are also deductible from your income taxes. VA loans, however, and other such loans backed by government sources are often not available for investment properties. Be sure you know the laws covering each type of loan you consider for investment purposes. You may consider using one type of loan for a home you purchase to live in and another for an investment.

Check your local newspaper and the Internet for information about rates and points currently being offered.

Ask for points to be quoted to you as a dollar amount—rather than just as the number of points—so you will actually know how much you will have to pay.

Fees

A home loan often involves many fees, such as loan-origination or underwriting fees, broker fees, and transaction, settlement, and closing costs. Every lender or broker should be able to give you an estimate of its fees. Many of these fees are negotiable. Some fees are paid when you apply for a loan (such as application and appraisal fees), and others are paid at closing. In some cases, you can borrow the money needed to pay these fees, but doing so will increase your loan amount and total costs. "No cost" loans are sometimes available, but they usually involve higher rates.

Ask what each fee includes. Several items may be lumped into one fee.

Ask for an explanation of any fee you do not understand. Some common fees associated with a home loan closing are listed on the "Mortgage Shopping Worksheet" in this book.

Down Payments and Private Mortgage Insurance

Some lenders require 20 percent of the home's purchase price as a down payment. Many lenders, however, now offer loans that require less than 20 percent down—sometimes as little as 5 percent on conventional loans. If a 20 percent down payment is not made, lenders usually require the home buyer to purchase private mortgage insurance (PMI) to protect the lender in case the home buyer fails to pay. When government-assisted programs such as FHA, VA, or Rural Development Services are available, the down-payment requirements may be substantially smaller. Again, with these types of loans, the purpose of the purchase may have limitations.

Ask about the lender's requirements for a down payment, including what you need to do to verify that funds for your down payment are available.

Ask your lender about special programs. If PMI is required for your loan, ask what the total cost of the insurance will be.

Ask how much your monthly payment will be when the PMI premium is included. Will the PMI end automatically when the principle owed reaches 80 percent of the loan/property value?

Obtain the Best Deal

Once you know what each lender has to offer, negotiate for the best deal you can. On any given day, lenders and brokers may offer different prices for the same loan terms to different consumers, even if those consumers have the same loan qualifications. The most likely reason for this difference is that loan officers and brokers are often allowed to keep some or all of this difference as extra compensation. Generally, the difference between the lowest available price for a loan and any higher price that the borrower agrees to pay is an overage. When overages occur, they are built into the prices quoted to consumers. If you can determine the overage, this may be a point for negotiation! They can occur in both fixed-rate and variable-rate loans and can be in the form of points, fees, or the interest rate. Whether quoted by a loan officer or a broker, any loan may contain overages.

Have the lender or broker write down all the costs associated with the loan. Then ask if the lender or broker will waive or reduce one or more of its fees or agree to a lower rate or fewer points. *You will want to make sure that the lender or broker is not agreeing to lower one fee while raising another or lowering the rate while raising points*. There's no harm in asking lenders or brokers if they can give better terms. Have all offers in writing to prove you have done your homework.

Once you are satisfied with the terms you have negotiated, you will want to obtain a written lock-in from the lender or broker. The lock-in should include the rate you have agreed upon, the period the lock-in lasts, and the number of points to be paid, if any. A fee may be charged for locking in the loan rate. This fee may be refundable at closing. Lock-ins can protect you from rate increases while your loan is being processed; if rates fall, however, you could end up with a less favorable rate. If that happens, try to negotiate a compromise with the lender or broker. Remember, they want you to get the loan. It is how they earn a living!

Remember: Shop, Compare, Negotiate

When you're buying a home, whether for your own occupation or as an investment property, remember to shop around, compare costs and terms, and negotiate for the best deal. Your local newspaper and the Internet are good places to start shopping for a loan. You can usually find information both on interest rates and points from several lenders. Since rates and points can change daily, you'll want to check your newspaper and Internet often. But the newspaper does not list fees, so be sure to ask lenders about them. They should be up to date on a daily, if not hourly, basis.

The Mortgage Shopping Worksheet in the back of this book may help you. Take a copy with you when you speak to each lender or broker and write down the information you obtain. Don't be afraid to make lenders and brokers compete with each other for your business by letting them know you are shopping for the best deal. In fact, taking this book along will show those with whom you are dealing that you have done serious investigation.

Fair Lending Is Required by Law

The Equal Credit Opportunity Act prohibits lenders from discriminating against credit applicants on the basis of race, color, religion, national origin, sex, marital status, and age. It doesn't matter where the applicant's income comes from, such as public assistance programs, or whether the applicant has in good faith exercised a right under the Consumer Credit Protection Act.

The Fair Housing Act prohibits discrimination in residential real-estate transactions on the basis of race, color, religion, sex, handicap, familial status, or national origin.

Because of these laws, a consumer cannot be *refused* a loan nor be *charged more* for a loan or *offered less favorable terms* based on such characteristics. Nor can they be offered more favorable terms because of their circumstances, even though some programs are designed to make it easier for lower-income earners to qualify.

Credit Problems? Shop, Compare, and Negotiate!

Minor credit problems or other difficulties stemming from unique circumstances, such as illness or temporary loss of income, military service, and other life events, will not necessarily limit your mortgage loan choices to high-cost lenders. If your credit report contains negative information that is accurate, but there are good reasons for trusting you to repay a loan, be sure to explain your situation to the lender or broker. You can even put notes in your credit report that lenders can see. Log into the three reporting agencies and explain negative information on their sites; this will be reflected each time your credit is pulled. If your credit problems cannot be explained, you will probably have to pay more than borrowers who have good credit histories. And if information in your credit report is inaccurate, take the steps to have it removed!

Don't assume that the only way to get credit is to pay a high price. Ask how your past credit history affects the price of your loan and what you would need to do to get a better price. Take the time to shop around and negotiate the best deal you can.

Whether you have credit problems or not, it's a good idea to review your credit report for accuracy and completeness before you apply for a loan. You are entitled to one free credit report per year, but it is best to get all three. To order a copy of your credit report, visit www.annualcreditreport.com, call 877-322-8228, or contact:

Equifax: (800) 685-1111

TransUnion: (800) 916-8800

Experian: (888) 397-3742

Chapter Five

Going to Bat

Caveat Emptor: "Let the buyer beware." The buyer must examine the goods or property and buy at his own risk, except for latent defects. Example: Often a property is offered "as is" with no expressed or implied guarantee of quality or condition. When entering such transactions, caveat emptor is a worthy admonishment.

When ready to buy, there is definitely an art to negotiating the fine points of real-estate transactions. Caveat emptor is the theme of this chapter, especially in regard to commercial properties. Knowing your opposing team's pitcher, his or her style, and what types of pitches to expect are all part of preparing to bat, even if you are already a seasoned batter and have spent time learning the proper techniques. Like practicing for your turn at bat, having a team you can trust to find issues and positive aspects of the property, such as future developments that may affect long-term value (good and bad), traffic patterns, or civil engineering perks and flaws, are all part of the research behind negotiation. And with negotiation, the contract begins to form.

All negotiation must be in writing. Phone calls should be documented and/or recorded, but the real negotiation must be on paper and signed by both parties and, if desired, notarized. Failing to cover all of your bases can leave you open to a runner stealing home. Though it would be great to think that everyone in business is honorable and playing by the rules, it just isn't always the case. Winning is the name of the game, and as in all business transactions, those who have the best seasons are the ones who consistently play to win.

Another term you must absolutely be clear on is *latent defect*, which means "a flaw or other imperfection in any article that is discovered after delivery; usually, latent defects are inherent weaknesses that normally are not detected by examination or routine tests, but that are present at time of manufacture and are aggravated by use."

This is like having a cracked bat, but you don't know it until you hit a foul, at best. At worst, the bat splinters during a third strike, and you're out. You can check for latent defects in a number of ways. Be sure to get into the property and ensure everything is in proper working order. Visit it after a storm or during a storm to check for leaks. Most important, know what's covered in your contract! When issues arise, handle them promptly. Do not delay if evidence of a problem appears. Call in the professionals: plumbers, electricians, contractors, and others. Since you already have your team ready to bat, it is your job to call them in when it is their turn to make the big plays.

Swinging the Bat before Stepping Up to the Plate

The purchase contract is such a vital part of the process that I recommend everyone has a professional look at each one. Even if you are a seasoned investor, another professional may catch something you don't. Just like having someone else edit written work, the best ballplayers always have coaches to help them improve. Contracts are legal documents. You can save yourself a lot of grief, time, and money by having another team member look over all contracts, even if you get to the point where you feel comfortable enough writing them on your own.

Be sure to familiarize yourself with all aspects of the game. Just as the viewers and fans in the stands and at home need to know the rules of baseball, the beginning investor should familiarize himself or herself with the contract essentials. The next section of this chapter lists these essentials and should be reviewed each time you enter into a contract. The best teams practice several times a week and just before the game. You should probably consider making a formal list for each new purchase and sale, since each one will have specifics to include and exclude. A generic list may omit something crucial, especially for an "as is" property or foreclosure.

Purchase Contracts

Preprinted purchase contracts may be convenient, but they may not be in your best interest. Purchase contracts are important documents and are the game plan for your transaction. You may want to use the sample forms to guide you, but you must have a clear understanding of everything contained. Read it entirely, especially the fine print. If you don't understand something, get help from a professional. Be very clear and have it explained to you so that you understand all of the implications. There may be wording to alert you to issues with the property that may not be fully disclosed elsewhere. Read between the lines and then ask questions to prompt full disclosure.

Easy to fill out preprinted forms may be intended to be neutral, but as a buyer, you may want be sure terms are listed that protect you! Real-estate professionals will often use contracts that make the closing easiest because this is when they get paid. Look out for your own interests when going over a purchase contract.

Typical of many such prepared contracts are arbitration clauses that make it less costly for the settlement of legal issues should any arise. Taking this option off the table puts you in a position of having no legal recourse should you disagree with the arbitrator's decision. Though one hopes to never need to go through such a process, situations arise that may require legal action. Because a clause is in the purchase agreement does not mean the contract is worthless. Negotiate. Ask to have it removed, reworded, or what your other options are in that instance. In fact, many real-estate attorneys will advise that you not agree to arbitration in the contract agreement. It is always an option to settle disputes this way—arbitration or even mediation—in order to avoid a lawsuit. Mediation allows you to try this process first and still have the option to file suit if an agreement cannot be reached.

Unless state or local laws require the clause, you have the right to change it. You can add to purchase agreements too. If something you want is not mentioned, indicate it, but remember to initial all changes and only sign the form once it states everything that you agree to and expect from the deal.

A good purchase contract will include very specific items, such as the property address and legal description. This will include boundaries and landmarks and even school district if that is something you're considering in your purchase decision. Be sure to know current zones, as school boundaries can change from year to year. Even if you intend to use the property as a rental, your tenants may want this information, and it can be a selling point for listing the property.

The contract will also include the names of the buyer and the seller. Though you will know all the players on the buyer side and will want to include them on the form, be sure that everyone whose name appears on the property's *title* is listed on the purchase contract too. All people listed will need to be present or represented at closing to ensure the title is properly transferred. A person who has not signed the official acceptance of the offer cannot be compelled to sign over the deed!

Earnest money is deposited when signing the purchase contract. Be sure the exact amount paid is listed on the agreement, which may range from a couple thousand dollars to 1 percent of the purchase price. Once your offer is accepted, the earnest money belongs to the seller if you back out, but is expected to be returned to you if the seller defaults. There may be other circumstances for retaining or returning the funds, so be certain you understand what all of these are.

Many contracts have specific reasons that allow for the return of the money, which is why you must protect yourself in this portion of the purchase agreement. You can choose where the money is to be kept, for example the escrow company, bank, or attorney, but upon closing, this money is part of your down payment. The contract should include all of the following items as applicable:

- Purchase price and terms of sale. Be very specific.

- Personal property. Some appliances and even window treatments or ceiling fans often are not conveyed. Ask for an itemized list.

- Provisions for seller's full disclosure of the property. Any defects that would affect the property's value. This includes information on what work has been performed on the property, such as structural repairs or additions and who performed the work. Was it a do-it-yourself addition or performed by a licensed contractor? Were all legal permits obtained for the addition or major renovation?

- Specifics on the *type* of deed to be given.

- Closing date.

- Closing costs specifically listing who pays for what and clearly itemized.
- Occupancy or possession date. If the seller is asking to remain in the property past the closing, this should be clearly stated, and terms agreed upon are also listed. If the buyer intends to move in or take possession prior to closing, this too would be stated and what financial agreements are expected at that time.
- All other contingencies or negotiated changes and in what time frame changes are expected to be complete.
- Seller's obligation to provide clear title.
- Title insurance, survey, termite inspections, and other fees and who will pay for these services.
- Proration agreements for adjusting taxes, rents, security and other deposits, fuel, water bills, and utilities between buyer and seller.
- Walk-through agreement and date for you to inspect the property for agreed-upon repairs, changes, or additions *prior to closing.*
- Requirements specific to the state.
- Date for the expiration of the agreement ideally one or two days after the contract is drawn up. Don't let this

> drag on too long, or you may find too many details have changed, such as financing options and real-estate market changes!

Give the seller time to respond, but be clear that you want an answer quickly as should be clear by the expiration date. Always be as specific as possible. Conflicts do arise but can be avoided by being clear in your communications and expectations. Problems can be avoided if one is proactive. It is not unreasonable to expect a prompt response. After all, this is a business transaction, whether you're buying from a professional investor or someone selling their only residence.

Buying from a Builder or Contractor

Builder contracts are intended to give the builder all the advantages and often contain red flags that may not be obvious to the novice investor or first-time buyer. Beware of signing these without the proper representation of a realtor or attorney. Builder contracts often include the right for them to "modify" your floor plan, making it "similar" to the plans or to "vary only slightly." A slight variation could be different materials or colors, and while this may seem "slight" to one person, it may be radically different to another. But in some cases, it could mean a change in room dimensions. Reducing the size of any room by only a couple square feet can make a big difference to the overall attraction of the property.

Builder contracts sometimes include the right on their part to replace certain components with "similar or better quality" items. Retain your right to be the one to make those decisions. No changes are to be made without your prior approval!

Builder contracts will also include additional fees due at closing. These may be special fees for infrastructural elements such as sewer and utilities or for amenities such as jogging paths or other items included in your homeowners' agreements. Be especially aware of any vague "closing fees" of 1 percent to 2 percent of the purchase price, which are often standard inclusions when purchasing directly from the builder. What do these fees cover? It isn't hard to do the math on those unexpected fees. A property of $200,000 would find $1,000 to $2,000 additional fees at closing!

Include some precautionary language such as "If seller does not presently hold title, this contract may be rescinded by the buyer." This is a time to include your attorney or realtor in the process of drawing up the contract. Even with reputable builders, you request a contract for your agent's or lawyer's approval. As with all contracts, don't get too emotionally attached. If any of your requirements are not met at least with negotiable solutions, be ready to walk away from the deal.

I am including a sample of a well-written contract to show how a purchaser can avoid pitfalls.

SAMPLE REAL ESTATE SALES AGREEMENT

This Agreement is entered into by and between ***[name of person selling the real estate]***, an individual with an address of ***[address of seller]*** ("Seller"), and ***[name of person/firm buying real estate]***, an individual with an address of ***[address of buyer]*** ("Buyer").

In consideration of the mutual covenants contained herein and other valuable consideration received, and with the intent to be legally bound, Seller and Buyer agree as follows:

1. SALE OF PREMISES. Seller agrees to sell and convey to Buyer, and Buyer agrees to purchase from Seller, the following Premises:

[legal description of property being sold].

The sale shall include all improvements and fixtures attached to the Premises and used in connection therewith, if any. The sale shall also include the following: ***[list any items of personal property included in sale, such as "one refrigerator"]***. The sale shall not include the following: ***[list items excluded from sale]***. Seller will deliver to Buyer on the closing a bill of sale for any personal property sold, which Seller guarantees is fully paid for.

2. PURCHASE PRICE. The purchase price for the Premises and any items of personal property is $***[purchase price of property, e.g. "$150,000.00"]***, payable on the closing as follows: ***[list how purchase price will be paid, e.g. "in cash," "$50,000.00 in cash, and $100,000.00 in mortgage to seller," or "$50,000.00 in cash, buyer***

to assume existing first mortgage in amount of $100,000.00," etc.]. All payments must be made with cash or certified funds. Seller acknowledges receipt from Buyer of a deposit in the sum of $***[list amount of deposit]*** to be held in escrow pending the closing. The deposit will be applied to the purchase price at the closing.

3. DEED. On the closing, Seller will convey the Premises by a good and sufficient ***[type of deed, such as quit claim or warranty]*** deed conveying a good and marketable title, free of all liens and encumbrances, except (i) all easements, rights of way, covenants, and restrictions of record, (ii) current and future real-estate taxes and assessments, (iii) zoning and other governmental laws and regulations, provided none of the foregoing interfere with the continued use of the Premises for its present use. Seller, at its sole cost, shall furnish Buyer with a preliminary report or abstract of title from a reputable title company within five (5) business days after the execution of this Agreement. Buyer shall give written notice to Seller of any objections to title within ten (10) days.

4. CLOSING. The deed will be delivered and the purchase price paid on ***[date sale will be finalized, such as "February 1, 2010"]***, unless extended in writing by the parties. The closing will be held at ***[list place the closing will take place]***. The sale will be closed according to the usual and customary closing procedures in effect in the county where the Premises is located. At the closing, Seller and Buyer agree to execute and deliver to the other all instruments required by law or which may reasonably be requested by the other party or the closing agent. The following closing costs will be paid by Seller: ***[list closing***

costs, if any, paid by buyer]. The following closing costs will be paid by Buyer: ***[closing costs, if any, paid by buyer].***

5. MECHANIC'S LIENS. At the closing, Seller will furnish to Buyer an affidavit attesting that no work has been performed on the Premises for which a mechanic's or materialman's lien could attach. If any work was performed on the Premises for which a lien has or may attach, Seller will obtain and deliver to Buyer appropriate lien waivers and releases executed by all contractors, subcontractors, and suppliers, in addition to the seller's affidavit.

6. DEFECTIVE TITLE. If Seller shall be unable to deliver title or make conveyance as provided herein, Buyer, at its option, may (i) terminate this Agreement whereupon the deposit shall be refunded to Buyer and all obligations of the parties shall cease, or (ii) waive the defects and accept whatever title Seller is able to convey, without any reduction in the purchase price and as a full performance by Seller.

7. POSSESSION. On the closing, the Premises and all improvements, fixtures and items of personal property, if any, will be delivered to Buyer in their present condition, reasonable wear and tear excepted. The Premises shall be free of all occupants, tenants, and personal possessions, except as may otherwise be provided herein. Buyer shall be allowed to inspect the Premises prior to the closing to determine whether the Premises complies with this section.

8. ADJUSTMENTS. Current property taxes, regular and special assessments, water and sewer charges, fuel, rents, interest, insurance, operating expenses, and other customary matters, if any, shall be prorated between the parties on the closing.

9. RISK OF LOSS. Seller, at its sole cost, shall keep the Premises insured for the full insurable value until the closing. Seller shall bear the risk of all loss or damage to the Premises from all causes until the closing. Should there be any damage that is not restored by Seller to its former condition by the closing, Buyer, at its option, may (i) terminate this Agreement and any deposit shall be refunded to Buyer, or (ii) purchase the Premises and be entitled to all insurance proceeds upon payment of the purchase price.

10. MORTGAGE CONTINGENCY. The obligations of Buyer under this Agreement are expressly subject to Buyer obtaining a written commitment for a mortgage loan in the amount of $***[list amount of mortgage buyer will seek to obtain]*** at prevailing interest rates. Buyer agrees to apply for such mortgage with all due diligence. If Buyer shall be unable to obtain such mortgage commitment by ***[list deadline for buyer to obtain mortgage] (note: Talk to your lender and make sure you give yourself time to get the loan commitment).*** Buyer shall inform Seller in writing by such date, and this Agreement will terminate and any deposit will be refunded to Buyer. If Buyer fails to notify Seller in writing by such date, Buyer shall be required to perform its obligations under this Agreement and this contingency shall lapse.

11. INSPECTION(S). ***(Often referred to as due diligence) Make sure you give yourself enough time to perform all the inspections you determine have to be performed.*** The obligations of Buyer under this Agreement are expressly subject to Buyer obtaining, at Buyer's expense, a satisfactory inspection report from a qualified

professional for the following: ***[list any inspections to be performed on property, such as "termites" or "termites and roof," "septic or sewer," "EPA phase 1" etc.]***. Buyer shall furnish Seller with a copy of such inspection report(s) by ***[date by which buyer must complete these inspections]. Make sure you notify the Seller of any defects before the expiration of your due diligence period.*** If any such inspections reveal conditions unacceptable to Buyer, Seller may, at its option, repair such conditions or afford Buyer a credit at the closing, or Buyer may terminate this Agreement, and any deposit will be refunded to Buyer. ***If problems are found, make sure that you give the Seller a specific time frame, typically five (5) business days, in which to respond.*** If Buyer fails to notify Seller in writing by such date, Buyer shall be required to perform its obligations under this Agreement and this contingency shall lapse.

12. BUYER'S DEFAULT. Upon default by Buyer, Seller, at its option, may (i) retain the deposit as liquidated damages as its sole remedy, or (ii) enforce this Agreement and pursue any and all remedies available at law or equity, including an action for specific performance and damages.

13. SELLER'S DEFAULT. Upon default by Seller, Buyer, at its option, may (i) treat this Agreement as terminated and be entitled to the return of the deposit, or (ii) enforce this Agreement and pursue any and all remedies available at law or equity, including an action for specific performance and damages.

14. BROKER'S COMMISSION. Seller and Buyer promise that they have not dealt with any broker or finder in connection with this sale. In the

event of any claim by any broker or finder, the party who procured such broker or finder will pay the claim in full.

15. ATTORNEY'S FEES. In the event of any litigation or other proceeding between the parties relating to this Agreement, the prevailing party shall be entitled to recover all costs and expenses incurred, including reasonable attorney's fees.

16. ENTIRE AGREEMENT. This Agreement contains the entire agreement and understanding between the parties and is subject to no understandings, conditions, or representations that are not set forth herein. This Agreement may only be amended in writing and signed by both parties. Time is of the essence in the performance of this Agreement.

17. JOINT AND SEVERAL LIABILITY. Each person signing this Agreement as Seller and Buyer shall be jointly and severally liable for the performance of every term and condition of this Agreement.

18. INVALID PROVISION. If any provision of this Agreement shall be invalid or unenforceable, the remaining provisions shall remain in full force and effect.

19. PARTIES BOUND. This Agreement shall be binding upon and shall inure to the benefit of the parties and their respective heirs, legal representatives, successors, and assigns.

20. GOVERNING LAW. This Agreement shall be governed by and enforced in accordance with the laws of the state of ***[list state which laws will govern the contract]***.

21. CAPTIONS. The captions in this Agreement are inserted only for convenience and in no way construe or interpret the provisions hereof or affect their scope or intent.

22. RELEASE BY SPOUSE. ***[list name of seller's spouse]***, spouse of ***[name of person selling the real estate]***, for consideration received, hereby agrees to join in the deed and waive and release all rights of dower, courtesy, homestead, community property, and all other right, title, and interest, if any, in and to the Premises.

23. ADDITIONAL PROVISIONS:

[list any other agreements between seller and buyer]

24. RIDERS. The riders and exhibits, if any, attached hereto and initialled by the parties are made a part of this Agreement.

THIS IS A BINDING LEGAL CONTRACT. IF ANY PROVISIONS ARE NOT UNDERSTOOD, CONSULT AN ATTORNEY BEFORE SIGNING.

IN WITNESS WHEREOF, this Agreement is executed under seal on the

____________ day of ____________ , 20 _____ .

Executed in the presence of:

SELLER

________________________ ________________________ (Seal)

(Signature of witness) ***[name of person selling the real estate]***

(Signature of witness)

________________________ (Seal)

[list name of seller's spouse]

BUYER

________________________ (Seal)

[name of person/firm buying real estate]

This contract would also include a notary's page with all relevant information required by law of the notary, including his or her seal. Before venturing off on your own with a form contract, compare it to the one I've included. Each property is unique as is each transaction.

Be sure to adjust your contract to the specifics of your situation to obtain the best possible deal. This is the most important inning of the real-estate ball game.

Investing in Commercial Property for Business

Investing in commercial properties is a totally different ball game. It's like the difference between playing Little League ball and playing in the pros. Many of the same techniques, habits, and terminology remain the same, but other things are vastly different. For example, in Little League, the batting lineup is determined by position played. Oftentimes we see a standard lineup of catcher, pitcher, first baseman, et cetera. But in the pros, the lineup is determined by many other factors. Understanding the differences in investing in commercial properties versus residential is also a new game with new rules. How the game plays out for each player and fan will be determined by the preparedness by the different team members.

Coaches understand the batting power of certain players, and that team member is then used in a specific position in the lineup to best use his talents. Like investing and other high-finance ventures, one must understand the numbers and the rules. Otherwise, it could spell disaster—or simply a poorly played game.

The most precious commodities in these times of serious investment considerations are commercial properties. And they require a lot of capital! Commercial properties are always expensive in comparison to agricultural or residential properties.

When planning to invest in a commercial property, there are some important factors to consider: legalities, forecasts of how it will generate income, and especially the capital required.

Legalities

The primary factor that needs to be examined when investing in a commercial property is the "legality" of your investment. Investigate all applicable local rules and laws, which might vary even within a city or county. These can be hard to understand, thus it might be useful to consult a lawyer who specializes in commercial properties and is familiar with local laws. There are often differences in the fine print from state to state and county to county, or even within municipalities.

Additionally, laws can change, so your legal counsel must have up-to-date knowledge. When you examine the property's legal aspects, view it from two angles: the legality of your investment in the commercial property and the legality of the commercial property itself. Spend some time looking into these aspects. Examine them not just twice but four times prior to making any big leaps. This will ensure the security of your investment.

Income-Generating Prospects

This second aspect is very important in making sure your investment will work for you. Based on present trends and future projections, you will need to ensure the property value will appreciate. This will make sure that if you need to sell it, you'll get more than what you paid for.

It's also vital that you consider what kind of income-generating prospects you'll have from the type of business you'll build or remodel on the property. Once more, legality will come into play. Various places have rules and regulations about the particular purpose land can be used for. In buying commercial properties, make certain you'll be able to legally utilize the property for your intended purpose.

Capital Required

Financing is one of the critical elements of any investment. It's not often that you will have all the capital required to invest in commercial properties. Thus, you'll probably need a commercial-property loan. Getting this kind of loan will require lots of documentation on one's business operations, one's financial status and potential for earning, and the title deed of the property, in order to convince the lending institution or individual that the money lent will be secured. This is very much like the difference between the salaries paid in the minor league versus those earned by professionals in the major league. The figures are much larger and require a lot more practice and effort on the part of all of the players on your team.

All lenders will require an appraisal of commercial property as they will on residential properties. This should be performed during the loan-contingency period. If the property doesn't appraise, your earnest deposit is refundable. Ensure that you're paying for a fair price. Prices that are too high will make you lose money, while low prices can be an indication something is wrong. Do your homework and don't be overly eager to push the deal through too quickly. The investment required for commercial properties is considerable, and thus an imprudent investment may financially ruin you.

In calculating the cash needed for a certain property, there will be some outside factors like closing and legal professional expenses and any registration fees. These can add up, and thus they must be included in your feasibility budget.

Shop around before settling on a property. Sometimes, the first property found isn't the best. After all, you wouldn't want to realize you've made a bad investment after putting in a down payment and signing all the needed paperwork.

Investing in commercial property is a good method for growing money, but not all people have been or can be successful at doing this. Therefore, it is important to take every necessary precaution.

There is no standard commercial purchase and sales agreement that will be perfect for all buyers and sellers or even for the same investor for different purchases and sales. Usually, buyers and sellers will change, delete, and add parts to the purchase and sale agreement to satisfy their needs for each specific transaction. Most often, however, buyers and sellers will get advice from a real-estate agent or an attorney. Understanding what you're doing before consulting a professional is a good idea, just as you might familiarize yourself with the terminology and lingo of any new sport. It can be frustrating for an American, for example, to attend a rugby match, because, though it looks similar to both soccer and football, the game, the rules, and the terminology are all different. One standard document is the Offer to Purchase Real Estate Agreement. This form is an offer and acceptance agreement form—offer and acceptance being the two essential parts of a valid contract.

Most offer-to-purchase real-estate agreements or letters of intent (LOI) are used as a preliminary agreement to set down the basic terms for the transaction. If the seller accepts the offer to purchase and the deposit, or earnest money, the buyer has the right to purchase the real estate for the terms listed in the agreement. This is not the actual purchase contract itself, which is one of the many forms used during the closing process, but it is part of the process itself. The LOI is simple and easy to use, but as I said earlier, each specific purchase or sale has its own details to consider. This agreement is designed to be quick and efficient. This enables the buyer to make an offer and get a faster response from the seller without filling out and reviewing a longer purchase agreement.

Once the agreement is accepted, the buyer and seller will usually follow up with a more detailed real-estate purchase agreement that defines the details of their transaction. With some shorter offer to purchase agreements, however, some buyers may choose to use it as a completed purchase agreement.

Chapter Six

Midseason Fitness

Have you ever known someone who was audited by the Internal Revenue Service and who really did not know they had done something illegal on their taxes? Ignorance of the law does not exempt one from the law. This is true in real estate, but it doesn't have to get to the point of breaking the law to find oneself in a losing game with no pinch hitters left.

Due diligence is your obligation as an investor. Most legal definitions of due diligence say something like "due diligence is a measure of prudence, activity, or assiduity, as is properly to be expected from, and ordinarily exercised by, a reasonable and prudent person under the particular circumstances; not measured by any absolute standard but depends on the relative facts of the special case." In other words, to a potential buyer, due diligence means making sure you get what you think you're paying for.

Practically speaking, for *any* acquisition, whether purchasing an item in an online auction or buying real property, due diligence includes fully understanding all of the obligations of the seller: debts, pending and potential lawsuits, leases, warranties, long-term customer agreements, any applicable contracts, distribution agreements, compensation arrangements, and so forth.

When it comes to investing your hard-earned money in real estate, due diligence is essential. Your real-estate agent and other members of your team should be able to assist you in this process, but it is of utmost importance that you participate. This is, after all, your investment.

Due diligence refers to a series of activities that will investigate the history of the property as well as the conditions of the sale and ownership of it. There is a lot to be done and often a short amount of time in which to do it. It should be done before or during the escrow process, during your inspection period, to determine if there are any physical (structural, electrical, mechanical, and plumbing), environmental, legal, or title problems, and to ensure full disclosure before you are at risk to lose your investment (earnest deposit).

The process can be started simply by obtaining a flyer or listing ad from the owner or agent. In today's real-estate market, online ads are plentiful and offer a wide range of disclosure. Check to see that the ad you saw is listed accurately. Then visit the property. Some listed properties may be vacant, and you can view the exterior on your own, but beware of violating someone's privacy if the home is still occupied. You can sometimes check with neighbors to see if the home is vacant.

When asking the neighbors, if this is appropriate, you may also be able to get a history on the home. Was the home abandoned? How was the property maintained? Were there extenuating circumstances causing it to go to foreclosure, for example? Sometimes the neighbors can give much insight into the care of the home or any major repair issues, such as flooding or roof damage. Was it ever used as a rental, and if so, how well was it maintained by renters and the landlord?

Viewing the interior will likely require entrance via the owner, occupant, or realtor. Be sure you are accompanied to avoid trespassing. You can't enter a property just because it appears vacant, even if it is unlocked. Be especially aware if there is a legal posting as these properties have specific legal ties or regulations. For example, properties that have been seized by and turned over for auction by the local sherriff or other legal authority will often have a notice prohibiting trespassing. Though these notices should be left clearly visible, you may still find yourself in trying to talk your way out of a sticky situation with a deputy. Again, do not enter a property without consent. You might, however, be able to gain consent by calling the owner or a realtor.

Owner information is public record. This type of information, if not posted in the yard or in an online advertisement or listing, can be obtained from the local or county assessor's office or perhaps via building permits. Especially with vacant and abandoned properties, or properties nearing foreclosure or auction, the owner may be very happy to hear from you. Timing is important, so knowing where the home stands legally is a good idea. Check local sheriff's auctions Websites to find properties. These are listed well in advance, and you can sometimes prevent the seller from losing it to repossession and get a good deal at the same time. Auctions are a great place to get properties, but winning auctions is a skill itself. It is difficult to get into the clique that attends auctions, but once you do, it is an excellent source of bird dogs and information on available properties. Auctions can be a great source for wholesale properties.

When contacting the owner, ask for the reasons behind the sale. It is important to know where the owner stands with the mortgage. If someone cannot afford to pay their house note, what other repairs and upkeep might they have neglected? Always get as much information about the owner and their situation as you can before an offer is made. Once you are comfortable with the information you have, you can make an offer.

Once the offer is made, you need additional information to continue with the process before the actual purchase itself. This would include an income and expense summary, especially for any kind of rental properties. This will help you project your cash flow. Along with this, you can request lease abstracts or summaries.

A site survey is appropriate to ask for at this point as well, since you will need to verify many things, such as property lines. Are all buildings and extra immovables located within the boundaries of the property? Is a neighbor's shed, building, or fence encroaching on the property? Verify this early on. You can then request that the seller or neighbor, for example, move the fence or storage shed to ensure it does not encroach on the subject property or an adjacent property.

The seller, too, should provide a property disclosure statement of pros and cons for the buyer. The seller should disclose any work and repairs made to the subject property. Inquire to find out if these were done by licensed contactors and, in the case of additions, that the proper permits were applied for and obtained. Check the age of the mechanical HVAC equipment (heating and air conditioning). If it is very old, there is a good chance you may have to replace it in the near future. The age of the subject property and how it has been maintained is a good indicator of what repair work or renovation will be necessary. Take all this in when calculating what you will pay for the subject property.

The laws of disclosure vary by state, and the forms are available online in PDF format for most states. Since I do most of my business in Arizona, I will cover what is typical for my state. I also think that it is an excellent place to invest for many reasons, including the laws of disclosure.

Even if you are not asked to do so, Arizona law requires that you disclose facts about the property, though the buyer or realtor will expect this from you. When completing a disclosure form, the Arizona statute on disclosure requires full disclosure regarding lead-based paint used in homes constructed prior to 1978, and if the property is in the vicinity of a military or public airport, this too must be clearly stated. You may find it useful to refer back to your own purchase agreement or other official forms you received when you purchased the property. Though requirements may have changed since you obtained it, the original documentation will be a good place to start looking for disclosure items.

If the buyer asks you about a certain aspect of the property, you have an obligation to relate the information, even if you do not consider the information relevant or important. Some things are important to some people and considered ridiculous by others. Like choosing paint and décor, we don't all agree on what's pretty or what's ugly. The same goes for disclosure, but in this case, the law has dictated certain parameters can decide if the buyer feels misled or lied to. If asked, you must disclose.

Also, it is necessary to prevent a previous statement from being misleading or misrepresented if something changes. On the other hand, you are not generally obliged to *correct* disclosed defects. These are negotiable items between you and the buyer. Again, you can be *sued* for not fully disclosing information on your property. It can be tantamount to fraud because nondisclosure is seen as an indication that a problem does not exist.

The Arizona Association of REALTORS® has a Seller's Property Disclosure Statement (SPDS), and it is specifically intended and designed to help you in fully disclosing everything to avoid unintentional nondisclosures. Remember, even if it was "an accident," you are still responsible for communicating facts as truthfully and as thoroughly as possible. I even suggest you attach copies of any available invoices, warranties for everything to be conveyed, even the five-year-old dishwasher no longer under warranty, inspection reports, and leases, to ensure that your information is accurate and complete. Use the blank lines to explain your answers. If you cannot answer a question on your own, don't guess! Consult a realtor or attorney if you have difficulty completing the form or are afraid you do not understand all of the specifics or expectations. Guard yourself from litigation from non-disclosure. Ignorance of the law does not make you innocent or "not guilty."

The SPDS form is available from your realtor or online, is easy to read, divided into six areas of disclosure, and is fairly self-explanatory. However, if you are unsure of what you must reveal, contact a realtor. The form goes on to list what does *not* need to be disclosed. This, however, does not necessarily prevent you from being asked them when selling or asking the owner or realtor these questions when you are the buyer. Arizona law does not require sellers to disclose that the property is or has been the site of death whether by natural causes, homicide, suicide, or any other felony. It also does not require the seller to disclose if the property was owned or occupied by a person exposed to HIV, or diagnosed as having AIDS or any other diseases not known "to be transmitted through common occupancy of real estate." Finally, even though this is a hot topic in the media and easily determined through Internet sources, you are not obliged to disclose if the property or residence is located in the vicinity of a registered sex offender. However, if you are asked these questions, it may be in your best interest to research this information on your own to prevent liability issues in the future.

The law does not protect a seller who makes an intentional misrepresentation. If you are asked about any of the situations above, you should not answer "no" or even "I don't know." Either answer truthfully or you can choose to say that you are not legally required to answer the question. Again, consult a professional if any such situations arise.

Note that the law does not protect against misrepresentation. If it matters to you that a death, for example, occurred on the property, put that in your list of standard questions to ask all sellers when you are shopping for investments. You should develop a list of questions to ask the seller, even after they offer the property disclosure statement.

At this point in your negotiations, you should not expect the seller to necessarily release information on title matters such as encroachments and easements, joint-use agreements or leases, liens and the status of them, or judgments. In addition, it is not the seller's obligation to disclose the financial demographics of the area or any other demographic matters. If the neighborhood has had an influx of a certain nationality or immigrant, it is your obligation to find out if and how the changing demographics are affecting the area, not the seller's.

If you are buying a rental property, it is also not the seller's obligation to reveal the credit worthiness of the tenants or their payment history or lease expirations. A motivated seller, however, might be willing to show you some of the items. Be careful not to violate a person's privacy. Until you own the building, you may not have the right to view such information under Federal Privacy Act laws. Know the laws or ask an attorney or professional property management firm that often operates as realtors as well.

There are some items that a motivated seller may *want* to share with you, such as expenses, deferred maintenance, outstanding loans, 1031 exchange, and a few others. But they are not obligated to do so.

Physical matters that you may want to investigate, if applicable and legal to do so, include traffic engineering issues. Is there road work in progress? This may initially hurt your investment in the short-term but help it in the long run. EPA phase 1 study and soil testing is important in most areas of the United States. This is something you can ask for, but it is not the seller's obligation to provide it. Consider parking issues, too. What type of property is it, and how many vehicles per dwelling would you expect to accommodate? Is there reasonable space? It is marked accordingly? What type of parking is there in the rest of the neighborhood? Do the neighbors seem to have ample room? Visit the property at various times to see the congestion and parking accommodations. Later in the evening and on weekends will show the highest number of vehicles home.

Also, if there are any engineering matters, whether electrical, mechanical, or environmental, these are not the obligation of the seller to disclose but still a good idea for you to investigate. For certain commercial properties, it is important to understand the zoning of an area and to know what you can and cannot use the property for. Is there a petition to rezone nearby buildings? This, again, is part of your own due diligence. The seller need not disclose it. You can ask, but often a person may not know. And when neighboring buildings, for example, in a residential area become rezoned commercial, the tendency is for the commercial zones to spread, especially on major thoroughfares and high-traffic-volume roads. Know what zones are near the property, even if it's easy to determine the zone of your purchase. Zones change. What happens, for example, if you don't conform to the zoning requirements? What permits are required if you are purchasing a commercial building in which you envision a convenience store or a beauty salon?

There are other matters to discover on your own or with the help of inspectors, contractors, or through public records. It may be possible to get a copy of the original architectural plans, with or without the materials specifications. From there you can determine if there were additions or upgrades, especially in neighborhoods built by the same contractor using only a few different plans. If this is the case, does your prospective property have upgrades or features that others in the neighborhood do not? Upgrades and unique features may be a selling point or they can be a hindrance. Odd floor plans or flamboyant fixtures may have been appealing to the previous residents, but tastes differ. How easily and cost-effectively can you change the aesthetic problems if they are severe? Be sure to keep flipping changes conservative and cost-effective. Making too many changes can quickly become expensive and eat up your profits before you know it.

Checking the roof is never to be skimped on. A professional roofing contractor might be necessary and can likely be hired at a minimal cost, but it is better to know before the first rainstorm if there is an issue with the roof. Roof issues, too, can reveal a host of other interior problems.

The overall structural condition and quality of the exterior can be assessed by an inspector who can also identify safety issues. Buildings of a certain age may not meet all current safety and fire regulations. This is especially important for commercial properties. But exterior is not the only aspect to be inspected. The mechanical systems of the property should be tested for their working condition and efficiency. Check the manufacture date of all mechanical equipment, ask for maintenance and repair schedules and copies of the maintenance contracts and repair bills. Replacing air conditioning units, heaters, and plumbing equipment and lines can be very costly. Be sure all toilets are flushed repeatedly, all showers and drains tested, and washing machines and dishwashers tested. Is the subject property on the public sewer or a septic system? Have them inspected. The cost to replace old "orangeburg" sewer pipe or leach lines on a septic system can be steep. If appliances are left, do they work? How old are they? When were they last serviced? Though the seller need not disclose this information, you can ask, and again, a motivated seller may wish to disclose such information.

New regulations on mold, whether environmental or caused by leaks from plumbing, are being implemented in most states. Know your state's regulations. Though the seller need not disclose this in the state of Arizona, if you intend to lease the property, it *is* your obligation to ensure these issues do not exist for your tenants. Know this before you sign at closing. Removing mold from a structure, whether residential or commercial, can be *very* costly and an environmental nightmare for those who must live or work in it. If the building(s) were constructed prior to 1978, they more than likely have asbestos. Talk to a qualified inspector if there is an asbestos problem.

Especially in regard to commercial real estate, know what utilities are necessary once your property is occupied. What are your obligations for the utilities and what will improvements, including gas lines and phone or cable, cost you? Are there any mandatory improvements you will be liable for?

In the course of your due diligence, what improvements will you make to the structure, if any? What types of contractors will you need? Are the improvements cosmetic or structural? How will these affect the value of your investment? One of the best ways to increase a property's value is to make minimally expensive improvements that give you a very high rate of return.

Finally, do you have the team members in place to give you the estimates for these improvements before you make your decision to buy? Be sure to ask how long it will take to make the suggested improvements if you decide to purchase the property in question. Time can be a big factor in turning the property around whether for resale or getting a tenant to occupy it. As you can see, you need to be able to call for help quickly. You are going to need a team of players who are ready to bat when you call them straight from the bench.

Chapter Seven

Playing the Game: When to Use the Relief Pitcher

Now that you know you *want* to buy the property, it is time to work up the sales contract. Writing the sales contract is one of the most important aspects in the actual purchase. Investors and home buyers can avoid many headaches with a well-written contract that covers all of the bases. Carefully written contracts provide protection for the buyer and seller. It is best done by professionals, at least in the beginning or until you are qualified. Remembering that each property has specifics that may need to be covered in the contract is the specialty of professional real-estate or other personnel. Be sure to include these players on your team and call upon them at the right moment. Always have contracts reviewed by a variety of professionals.

Remember that the sales contract is a negotiation. *Ask for what you want.* You can always counteroffer any rejection. But you are not likely to get what you want if you do not ask. Negotiation in any business arrangement or agreement is an art. Practice is going to pay off and produce winning results, so learn to do it well. The following section gives tips for just such bargaining. Though it approaches the topic from the seller's point of view, it also gives a buyer excellent ideas about what it is *good* to ask of a seller and what may be over the top. But remember, motivated sellers may be willing to do things you might not normally consider asking for. It is a negotiation. It's business.

The Art of Negotiating a Real-Estate Contract

It seems simple enough to say, "Don't lose your shirt." All joking aside, most people don't know how to negotiate a contract, or at least one they won't regret later. So here are some guidelines to making a sound decision while making some money.

This information is intended is for sellers. If you're making a purchase, just reverse the ideas. These are very black-and-white suggestions, so don't attempt to make them more complicated just because you want something today that you might not want next week.

There are simple steps to winning in negotiation. This is a business transaction. Keep your cool. Keep your temper and emotions under control. How do you do that? Well, the first step is to remove yourself from the idea that you might be selling your home to someone you don't like, that the neighbors won't like, or someone you said you would never sell your home to. Ignore all of those feelings. Put any judgments about people aside. Leave all prejudices at the curb. Most buyers who are interested in your home *can* afford your home, and with certain guidelines stipulated in the contract, you will soon find out if they will buy or not.

Look at all monetary concessions as just that: a concession. Figure your bottom net with the money that is offered. Don't forget that you will most likely have a negotiation period and that you might give up some more money after the inspection. Use your gut instincts to figure out what that amount might be, or even better, have your home inspected *before you put it on the market* so that you know what you can expect and you can have any necessary repairs made prior to entering into a contract. When you make repairs prior to attracting a buyer, they can be scheduled with the contractor of your choice and not just someone who's available, and at a predetermined price, not one set with you needing to close in two weeks or sooner!

Don't take the buyer's requests that are personal too seriously. This goes with the next step. For example, many times buyers request that the home be professionally cleaned. This does not mean that you or your wife, who has stayed home and kept a tidy house for the last twenty years, is a bad housekeeper. Just figure in the amount of money that it will take to bring in a cleaning crew and add it as a concession.

Focus on your selling price and bridging in the middle with the buyer instead of quibbling over all of the nitpicky stuff. For instance, if you are asking $250,000, and the buyer makes an offer at $230,000, and you can really sell for $240,000, figure in all of the concessions and make an offer that will yield you $240,000, but make sure that you *list* the concessions and how much they are worth to you. An example may be if the buyer wants your new refrigerator. You may have paid $1,800 for it new and figure it is worth $1,250 now. List that for the buyer to see.

If the buyer really wants a closing date that will be inconvenient for you, consider moving the date if they pay more. You may find yourself moving into temporary housing, which will affect your net profit.

Home warranties help with the negotiation of inspection items. Make sure you know this is an option and what it covers. Most home warranties have a deductible of around $55 per occurrence. For example, if you have a hot water heater that is old but still works, and the buyer is asking for a replacement, tell them you will pay for the warranty and give them an additional $220 for four repair visits under the warranty.

Anything you have to say to the buyer should be on a cover sheet with your counteroffer and faxed with the offer. It should never be left for your agent to translate. Speak to your buyer directly when you can. Your realtor should be present, but if you can speak directly to the buyer, the risk of something being missed or miscommunicated is lessened.

You may consider trying to make the buyer feel good by offering to serve them lunch or coffee during the inspection. Tell them you want to share all the important and interesting things about the neighborhood and that you will ask your neighbors on the right and left sides to come over and introduce themselves at that time. They're moving into a home. Feeling welcomed in advance will make minor bumps in the road less frustrating for them.

Any qualification for a loan should be rushed, and if the buyer is already approved, not preapproved, you should consider taking less money for the house (just a little) and treat this buyer with kid gloves. I know this counteracts some of what I said earlier, but it makes better sense when you are in the transaction. Many real-estate deals fall through when contracts are signed without loans fully approved.

Use very tight time frames so that your buyer does not cool off and reconsider. You want them to remain enthused about buying the property *you* are selling and not one that may pop up in the meantime. They need to remain committed, and this may take effort on your part. This is why having them enjoy a meal or coffee in your home and developing friendships with their new neighbors can be a big plus. It keeps them excited. You really have to focus during this time to push the contract through to binding. If your agent agrees, ask them to conference call you and the buyer's agent and possibly the buyer to talk about any issues. That way there is no resentment about what might not have been said. Your wishes will be clearly conveyed to all parties. Again, nothing will get lost in the translation.

Remember that negotiating is fun and should not be stressful. If you are stressed, you are either judging the buyer, not looking at the transaction as a bottom-line net, or you are taking the special stipulations or requests too seriously. Relax and see it as a game. Each inning is played as a step toward winning the game and going to the playoffs, and maybe even to the World Series for the serious investor!

How to Write Better Real-Estate Contracts

Wise people in all professions know that we must always look for ways to improve. The universe is in a constant state of flux. Things change. Laws change. Situations are all different, especially in real estate. Remaining willing to learn to do things better and more efficiently is the mark of a good businessperson. This certainly applies to pros and novices when it comes to writing better real-estate contracts. Always remain teachable.

As a REALTOR®, I know that a lot of time can be spent trying to convince clients that their real-estate contracts are not long enough or inclusive of enough specifics. Most people want to keep it simple—just want a one-page, simple, and easy-to-read and understand contract. It's often in their best interest to include more details, not less, to the agreement they are hoping the buyers or sellers will accept. I'm frequently met with resistance. Their intention is clear: just close my deal.

An example of why being more specific when writing real-estate investment contracts is better is the inclusion of clauses mandating the retention of liability and damage insurance coverage. When, for example, contracts don't require the buyer to maintain any liability or damage coverage on the property, this can be a dangerous situation during the transition process. If you're the seller, unless you're willing to provide the coverage, which is not often the case, then the contract needs to legally require the buyer to do so. It's not enough that the purchaser actually shows proof of the coverage because coverage can be cancelled at any time with a simple call to the insurance agent. This issue should be clearly stated in the purchase agreement.

Plan Ahead for Breach of Contract

Oftentimes, buyers get so emotionally wrapped up in this one being the perfect property, deal, or location that they fail to see the dangers to their financial life. A bad real-estate deal can destroy much of your portfolio, depending on what you have invested. Always remain willing to walk away from the deal. A good ballplayer knows when to return to the locker room, reschedule a game for a "rain out" even if the game is well under way or even to forfeit if it comes to that. One way to allow yourself to reschedule the game is to be sure your financing includes a contingency clause that allows you to get out of the contract should you not be able to get financing. "Board of Realtors" purchase and sales agreements in many states have language on this issue, which is really in favor of the seller because financing is becoming harder and harder to obtain for some. But this makes it harder for a buyer to walk off the field or walk away from the deal.

Another item to consider is to be very certain that the person or people with whom you are negotiating have the legal right to do so. If you are buying from a corporation, what is the standing of that company? Are they currently involved in any litigation or lawsuits that may affect your property? Who or what entity owns the title to the property or land? Check all provisions carefully. Do your homework or have trusted team members do the research for you before putting any earnest money down or signing anything!

Reserving Earnest Money

If you are acting as a buyer on a real-estate deal, you want to be sure that your contract protects your right to get that money refunded to you except in the case of an outright breach of contract by you. Not many of us ever intend to break the contracts we sign, but things happen when we do decide to leave the game. Be sure to make specific provisions for the return of your money. If you're a seller, however, you may feel differently for returning the money of a potential buyer you feel may not have been playing fairly. It is a judgment call, so learn to write these clauses in with the help of professionals who've seen all types of plays made in this area.

Earnest money is put in escrow to show you're a serious buyer. But sellers often get very attached to that money and feel that, no matter what, they deserve it even if they cause the closing to fall through. Specifics on the way earnest money is kept or not needs to be spelled out very clearly.

Appraisal Is Everything!

Having the correct team member write the contract and include everything possible is the best game plan. Much attention needs to be placed on the wording of the appraisal provision. It is important. Buyers should always include a provision that the entire contract is contingent on the property appraising for at least the purchase amount, or you could find yourself required to put down more money to secure financing!

In a nutshell, what is *not* stated in the contract is just as important if not more so than what *is* listed. Is everything you know about your verbal agreement clearly written as well? Though a purchase or sales agreement may state things that never come up, it's like preparing for maneuvers from the other team. Just because you don't know what pitch is coming at you when the pitcher stands on the mound, you still must know how to swing at the ball coming at you or choose not to swing at all, if it is outside the strike zone. Practice, get coaching, and be prepared with your own equipment before entering the field.

Valid Contracts Written on What?

Time is often of the essence in real estate. Being in the right place at the right time and being well prepared can be the difference of winning the game or forfeiting. Having a sample form may be better to begin negotiation because you can alter a sample form and initial intended changes then have other professionals look it over while the other party does the same. Preparedness is much more impressive, and buyers and sellers alike will see you're serious, but if you're in a pinch, something in writing is better than a verbal agreement. "Even if your real estate contract has been written on toilet paper, it's valid," according to Dr. Phil Speer. Though this is certainly amusing, it is something to consider. I suggest, however, keeping at least a legal pad handy, as it appears more professional—but with the accessibility of laptops and portable printers, it is easy to create contingent contracts on paper on the spot. Speer's article on www.ezinearticles.com, entitled "Real Estate Investing Contracts on Toilet Paper," tells us that the "content of your real estate investing contract is what's important." This shows that there are quick ways to get a contract under way when time is of the essence. The reason he says this is because "[y]our financial destiny in real estate investing is sealed BEFORE you walk into a real estate closing as a buyer.... The payoff of the transaction under anticipation is predetermined when the contract is signed between you as the buyer and the other party who is the seller." If this is the case, which indeed it usually is, it is in order to increase profits that we want to enter into this with confidence and preparedness.

This is the biggest reason for having your *own* preformed contracts available to you on a laptop that, as you begin to learn to negotiate more comfortably, you can then add the specifics to for the deals you are negotiating and have it reviewed by your attorney or other real-estate professional. Having access to your own forms may give you an edge in a moment or two. This can show that you are serious and are ready to move quickly. Contracts can be written with the phrase "contingent upon" added to them and then revised. It shows eagerness and serious investor skills. When writing contracts, understand that everything is negotiable. Though there is protocol typically followed for the payment of certain closing costs, you are not bound by it. Financing and seller motivation may eliminate some costs for you. Be sure to look at the big picture and take your cash-on-hand situation into account when negotiating. If you fail to state this in your contract, the closing agent, attorney, or title company, will simply use customary closing protocol. State it in writing so that everyone involved is clear on who is to pay for what.

It is not difficult to see where resorting to customary convention is not always in anyone's best interest. We must always adapt our contracts to the specifics of each deal, and each contract evolves due to the nature of the transaction. Since everything is negotiable, or many things are, having a form from a local office supply house is not going to serve you when trying to negotiate and move quickly. But learning to write your own and having the technology available on the spot will! However, this is not to be done by the novice. The purpose of this book is to form a team that allows you to be the coach, manager, and, if need be, a player who can pitch or catch, too! Good coaches have played the game and most of the positions too.

One of the best feelings in the real-estate business is leaving the transaction with a large check made payable to you. This is more likely to happen when you control the negotiations from the beginning and choose wording in contracts to prevent surprise fees, repairs, or obligatory services such as covering liability insurance premiums or being responsible for utilities and taxes, which you can find will be quickly eating away your profits.

Every investor, whether in real estate, the stock market, or any other market, is in the game to make money. Our society is moving back toward using more cash, so creating a cash flow through real-estate investing, using ethical and legal means, will put you and your investing team in a much more stable financial position. Housing is always a necessity. We may go to electric or hydroelectric cars, or do away with outdated technology such as fax machines, but real property is a market that will always have buyers and sellers, no matter what happens in other areas of our economy. Are you ready to create the cash that gives you the edge if the banking industry makes obtaining mortgages too difficult to obtain? I do not see that happening, but should it, having cash will ensure that you can continue to invest in real property.

When one begins to earn large amounts of cash, legal issues arise like never before. We've become a culture of litigates. Everyone, no matter their financial or family situation, usually has an attorney they use—even for finding a different attorney! Family attorneys may point you to a criminal attorney or real-estate attorney. Some in our society still misinterpret Shakespeare's famous line "first we kill all the lawyers." The irony here is this statement is uttered because the antagonists are contemplating overthrowing the government. Attorneys can also be good. The bard also said, "A friend in the court is worth a penny in purse." So how do we decide when to use an attorney in real-estate investing and when it is not necessary?

A Real-Estate Closing Attorney versus a Title/Escrow Company

There is always more than one opinion on a particular topic. Whether you should use an attorney versus a realtor depends on your experience in real estate. The other deciding factor may be determined by the laws of the state where you're purchasing the property.

Attorneys are not required for real-estate closings in all states. In fact, many states allow title companies to complete these transactions so real-estate attorneys are not often involved in simple transactions such as the purchase of single family homes for occupation by the owner or raw land transfers. This will save money on closing costs, as attorney fees are typically higher. You should always investigate the title company and ensure they are licensed to operate in the state where the property is located. Check the escrow officer's qualifications, as this requires a license as well. Companies that operate nationwide are good to use especially if you invest in a variety of states or those outside your domicile. This will allow you to develop a relationship with them and conduct all of your transactions efficiently. You *can* have your attorney involved in the process, if you desire.

Closings bring all parties involved in the transaction together simultaneously to expedite the transfer of title, which is only done once the settlement of all costs is complete. In the same meeting, the closing will deliver all documents to both buyers and sellers or their representatives. This is not a simple process and requires a thorough knowledge of all applicable laws. Sellers and purchasers often turn to lawyers due to the complexity.

Whether handled by a lawyer or title company, a closing involves the examination of the title, completion of the explanation of legal documents, and resolution of any of the possible title difficulties. In some states, real-estate closing attorneys are required to conduct each of these steps. First they examine the title records for prior conveyances, unpaid mortgages, liens, judgments, easements, and other encumbrances and clouds on title. They verify the authority of the seller to convey a good title to the property free of errors in its entire chain, which can, in some cases go back many years and through questionable transitions. This can be very tedious and should be done by someone trained to look for errors and omissions. Real-estate attorneys will also negotiate with the title insurance company for insurance coverage against any adverse claims of ownership, liens, and easements should they be filed once you have possession of the property.

Whether you use an escrow company or attorney, the closing authority will next combine all relevant information into one set of documents. At the closing, they also provide detailed explanations to ensure that both the buyer and seller understand all the issues involved in the sale. This includes the relevant contracts of sale, obligations of contracts, ordering of the title searches, analysis of title searches, significance of the title search, quality of the title, extent of risks, probability of damage, obligation to close or not to close, the process of closing itself, and documents exchanged. They then disburse funds, record relevant documents as public records, and prepare title-insurance policies for the buyer and lender.

The escrow company's or attorney's roles can be summed up as follows:

For buyers, they:

- Approve and negotiate the specific terms of all contracts (realtors or attorneys)
- Assist the buyer in the understanding of financing agreement (realtors or attorneys)
- Evaluate all legal documents, such as the deed, title policy, mortgage, survey, closing statement, and seller disclosure statement for clear conveyance, coverage, etc.
- Attend the closing
- Review all charges to ensure they are consistent with estimates given
- Provide updates of issues that affect the property and provide counsel and representation if difficulties arise

For sellers, they:

- Approve and negotiate the specific terms of all contracts (realtors or attorneys)
- Request title searches, surveys, mortgage-payoff letters, condominium documents, and all other necessary items handled in closing
- Prepare all other closing documents, including the deed and closing figures
- Arrange for the closing at a convenient time and place for all parties involved
- Attend the closing and ensure that a clear title is conveyed and that the seller is released of all obligations connected with the property
- Review all charges to ensure sure they are consistent with estimates given

Early in chapter 1, I discussed the importance of using a 1031 exchange agent. Please keep in mind that this is the job of a professional. However, as always, it is a good idea to know what the process is. There are five steps involved in a successful 1031 tax-deferred exchange, which can help you defer a significant amount of money in capital gains taxes.

This process will be easier to understand once you've done it a few times, but there are basically five steps to completing a 1031 tax-deferred exchange. The first is to properly list your property with a real-estate broker. The listing must specify that you intend to use it as a 1031 exchange. Again, it is important to have these players on your team who will help ensure that you "have your bases covered."

The second step involves the sales contract. Once you have a buyer, this step is standard procedure for any real-estate transaction and in addition to all provisions in that well-written contract mentioned earlier, and you will either agree to the offer or counteroffer. Once you and your buyer are in agreement, you must be clear that you intend to use this property as a tax-deferred exchange. This is to be part of accepting the terms of the agreement as you are required to intend to acquire a new property to satisfy Section 1031 of the Internal Revenue Service code.

The third step in this process is different from other real-estate transactions as you will need to begin working with a facilitator who will prepare the 1031, exchange documents. You will also need to open an escrow account, and your 1031 exchange agent will work with the escrow company too. The exchange agreement must be signed by everyone involved, and all earnest money must be deposited with the title company before closing the escrow.

Finding a replacement property is step number four. You have 45 days from the closing of the sale of the property you sold to find it, but you have 180 days to close on it. It is vital that everyone concerned knows that it too is part of a 1031 tax-deferred exchange.

The final and fifth step in this process is closing on the replacement property. You'll open a new escrow account for this property, and the facilitator will begin preparation of the documents required in the second step. Your earnest money will be held in the escrow account by the facilitator until all transactions are closed.

There are other situations that can arise during a 1031 exchange, so it's important that you seek the help and advice of your team members to ensure you're complying with the law during each phase of this process. There can be large amounts of money involved here, and failing to comply with the law can result in hefty fines at tax time, especially because you are also allowed to exchange your current property for several new properties. The rule of thumb for this is that the new properties' value cannot exceed 200 percent of the value of the property you sold to begin this exchange process.

Properties involved in a 1031 exchange must also be of a like kind, meaning that they will be used in a business or investment capacity. There are also some time constraints as to when you can claim the exchange on your income taxes, so as always, it's best to check with your various professional advisors before you begin the 1031 exchange process. You cannot play the game alone. You must have a full roster, including pinch hitters and relief pitchers. Though all transactions may not use the same members of your team, it's crucial to know when to make the best use of the talents of your lineup.

When to sell involves as much risk as making the purchase. But learning the market and moving according to your own research and the advice of your team will make this gamble safer. First you must decide when to sell—or at least list—the property for sale. Then the price and terms of the sale are to be considered. Are you selling through a realtor, and if so, what commissions are involved? Perhaps you will do it yourself (for sale by owner, or FSBO). If you choose this option, there are many ways to market the home online, in the printed media, or even on cable channels. What incentives will you offer? And what selling strategies will you use to market the property or showcase it for sale? Finally, what will you do with the proceeds from the transaction, such as transition the funds into another property, 1031 exchange, or even put the money into a totally unrelated account or investment? This is where you will need several of your team members, even if you chose to sell it yourself.

Sales team members include a bird dog (scout) to find the properties in competition with yours. This is extremely helpful since you may have a property of equal value, but the schools nearby may be a better selling point. Your knowledge of what properties are on the market and at what price points needs to be updated daily. A real-estate agent, real-estate broker, wholesaler, partner, lease-option tenant, property manager, or any other team member are possible leads to a potential buyer. Networking is the key to successful selling.

Chapter Eight

Winning the Trophy

Closing real-estate transactions can be one of the most stressful moments for the average home buyer, but it is the desired result, just like the trophy and prize money for professional athletes. Here, I want to show you some of the best ways to take ownership and reveal some expectations of the process. Knowing the terms of closing, being prepared, and choosing the appropriate times, dates, and professional services can make this normally stressful process much easier. Did you know you can use "by proxy" signers and closers? You do not actually have to be *at* closing when you have the right players on your team. Some real-estate investments are best made in other states, or you may have unforeseen circumstances arise that prevent you from attending the closing. The information in this chapter can help facilitate the process, providing you can trust your team members to take a turn at bat and allow you to enjoy the game from the stands. It is important to keep in mind how to overcome issues, which is why I stress the need for the *team* of professionals, especially in the last inning.

On October 3, 1951, New York Giants outfielder Bobby Thompson hit the shot heard 'round the world to end one of the most famous baseball games in history. Thompson made his game-winning hit off Brooklyn Dodgers' pitcher Ralph Branca at the Polo Grounds to win the National League pennant. True baseball enthusiasts know the time as 3:58 pm. As a result of Thomson's home run, the Giants won the game by one run, with a score of five to four over the Dodgers. They won the tiebreaker series two games to one. It was an exciting game overall, but the last inning was especially thrilling and has gone down in not just baseball history but broadcasting history as well.

The phrase "the shot heard 'round the world" is actually from a poem by Emerson, which depicted the first exchange during the American Revolutionary War. It has since been used in dramatic moments, such as this historic pennant game between the Dodgers and the Giants, and we often hear it used in business, which has borrowed heavily from baseball terminology. Phrases like "home run" and "team player" can easily shift from one application to another. In the case of Thomson's home run, it was particularly vivid because U.S. troops fighting the Korean War listened to radio broadcasts of the game. Indeed, this game was heard 'round the world.

The calling or announcing of the game was as famous—maybe even more famous—than the game itself because few American homes had television. The broadcast has been recorded, saved, and cited many times. The broadcasters are admired for their professional engagement with the audience and their description of the action, as well as the excitement that drove home the winning moment.

Thomson's home run and the Giants' subsequent victory, after overcoming a double-digit lead by the Dodgers in the weeks prior to the playoff, are known as the Miracle of Coogans' Bluff. This was a game, a moment in history, when something spectacular came at the last minute and changed the overall outcome. My point in bringing up this game is to encourage you to persevere in what may seem to be a daunting process—that of the real-estate closing.

That game was not a playoff game in the current postseason sense, but an extension of the regular season—game statistics counted in the season records. It had to be played because the Giants and their crosstown rivals, the Brooklyn Dodgers, finished the regular season with identical 96–58 records.

By early August, Brooklyn held a 13 ½ game lead on the Giants, but the Giants turned around and won their next 16 games, kicking off a winning streak in which they won 37 of their next 44 games, including the last 7. This is almost unheard of in baseball, especially in 1951. Only a 14-inning victory over the Philadelphia Phillies, the previous year's champions, on the last day of the regular season enabled the Dodgers to force the best-of-three-games showdown.

Brooklyn won the coin toss to decide the home-field advantage. In a surprising and controversial move, Dodger manager Charlie Dressen opted to play only the first game at home, rather than the last two, rationalizing that if his team won their home game, they would only need to win one out of the two on the road.

The Giants won the first game, 3–1. This blew Dressen's home-field strategy. When the series moved over to the Polo Grounds, the Dodgers won the second game in a 10–0 shutout with rookie pitcher Clem Labine.

For the third game, the Giants' 23-game winner Sal Maglie faced Brooklyn's Don Newcombe in a battle of aces. The top pitchers faced each other. In the first inning, Jackie Robinson singled home Pee Wee Reese for the first run of the game. In the bottom of the seventh, Thomson tied the game with a sacrifice fly, scoring Monte Irvin. In the eighth, the Dodgers touched the exhausted Maglie for three runs and headed to the bottom of the ninth with an apparently secure 4–1 lead.

Newcombe, however, was showing the effects of overuse in the season's final days. He had pitched the entire game the previous Saturday, then threw almost six innings the next day in the season finale. Pitching on only two days' rest and tiring badly, he attempted to take himself out of the game, only to have Robinson talk him into trying to finish. This is a good thing to keep in mind in your own game. Know when to call in relief. Sometimes team members may be overworked, and it is a good idea to know what is going on with your team players. If an attorney is overworked, for example, and shows signs of fatigue or inattentiveness, it may be time to use another, even if only for one occasion.

A single by Giants' shortstop Alvin Dark signalled a rally that moved the game along quickly. This young man attended Louisiana State University in 1942, where he played baseball for the Tigers, a well-known team of winners who made it to the College World Series. Interestingly, there is a street named for him in the predominantly student housing area of Baton Rouge, Louisiana, where multiunit houses and apartments are located. Now his name is associated with real estate. Every area has a history, and knowing that history may be vital to your venture, or even just for fun.

The Dodgers may have made a crucial strategic mistake at this point. First baseman Gil Hodges was playing close to the base, but with a three-run lead, the normal strategy would be to position for a possible double play. With a large gap in the right side of the infield, Don Mueller placed a single through that gap, past the diving Gil Hodges, and Alvin Dark ran from first to third base. Instead of a possible rally-killing double play, the Dodgers found themselves facing the potential tying run with no outs. But with a chance to drive in a run, Irvin, who led the National League that year with 121 RBIs, chased the first pitch and his pop fly was caught. He was out.

Whitey Lockman followed with a double down the left-field line, scoring Dark and advancing Mueller to third. Mueller slid awkwardly into the bag and broke his ankle, forcing the Giants to send in Clint Hartung to pinch run. Dressen, the Brooklyn manager, finally pulled Newcombe, at this point totally spent, and sent in Ralph Branca. This move has bewildered baseball fans and historians and added to other questionable decisions in that inning. Branca had pitched and lost Game One of the tiebreaker and had given up several home runs that year to Thomson, who had hit 31 during the season. But none of the Dodgers pitchers were sufficiently rested.

Branca's first pitch was a fastball down the middle for a strike. His second pitch was a fastball up and into Thomson, who yanked it just inside the foul line—with a dramatic dash by Andy Pafko, the Dodger's left fielder—and into the stands for a game-ending three-run homer. With just a swing of the bat, Thomson turned near-certain defeat into sudden victory and a pennant.

As the ball disappeared over the fence, Thomson leapt around the bases while the fans cheered wildly. He was swamped by his team at home. The stunned Dodgers left the field in utter disbelief and dismay. Waiting to bat next was a man who would become known for his own home runs, the 22-year-old Willie Mays.

Four broadcasters captured the moment for baseball fans nationwide. These men were as instrumental in bringing this historical event to the American public as were the players, coaches, and managers themselves. Perhaps even more so. It is important to understand that success may come from some of your most unsuspecting team members.

Ernie Harwell's call on Giants TV flagship station WPIX—carried nationally on the NBC television network—was a simple "It's gone!" belted out almost concurrently with the strike of the bat. Harwell later admitted he had probably called it "too soon," but fortunately it proved correct.

Meanwhile, the Dodger's radio voice, Red Barber of WMGM-AM, straightforwardly said, "Branca pumps, delivers, a curve, swung on and belted, deep shot to left field … it is … a HOME RUN! And the New York Giants win the National League pennant and the Polo Grounds go wild!" Barber, who was known for a relatively low-key, play-by-play approach, later criticized the famous Hodges rendition, which follows, as "questionable journalism," but it is probably the most famous coverage of the event.

Russ Hodges, broadcasting from WMCA-AM radio for Giants fans, seemed to be the least likely man to immortalize the play; he was a local announcer and not a national voice, and Hodges was considered calm-voiced rather than excitable. Nonetheless, it was his call that captured the suddenness and exultation of the Shot Heard 'Round the World. You can see it on YouTube (www.youtube.com/watch?v=lrl7dVj90zs).

The proper use of team members, coaching, practice, and determination, combined with creativity, can produce wonders in real-estate investing or any other venture. Being able to see things in alternative ways can help you find solutions to your dilemmas. In real estate, as in other ventures, things can appear out of the blue, or they can take time and determination and go into extra innings. But as long as you're in the game, you're still winning.

The following is from Bob Proctor's "Insight of the Day," a daily inspirational email. I think it is appropriate to include it in this chapter because it shows that creativity is so important in the world of business, whether you are a real-estate investor, athlete, entrepreneur, or banker. Bob writes:

> *I have often wondered why most companies have a creative department with a limited number of people, usually a very small percentage of the people that are on the payroll.*
>
> *Every department in a company is a creative department as long as the department has people in it. All people are creative. Creativity has its root in the Creator that is within each of us. As you permit the higher side of your nature to express itself in a greater way for good in your life, you are being creative.*
>
> *There are an enormous number of people who deprive themselves of many of the joys life offers because they believe they are not creative.*
>
> *"Musicians are creative, writers, artists and designers are creative, but I'm not."*
>
> *You should realize there are creative auto mechanics, carpenters, secretaries, and warehouse people. There are lawyers, accountants, and dentists who are creative.*
>
> *Creativity has absolutely nothing to do with what you do, but it has everything to do with how you do it. William James said, "Creativity is the ability to think in unhabitual ways."*
>
> *Pay particular attention today to the various people you*

come in contact with. Observe closely how these people apply themselves to their jobs.

Some will be an absolute symphony in every move they make. It will be obvious they have given creative thought to their work, while others move in a very mechanical way. If they are asked to do anything that may be out of the norm, you may very well hear the reply, "I'm sorry, that is not my job." There are definite self-imposed limitations to their activity.

They have never learned that they are a truly dynamic being with limitless creative potential in every fiber of their beings. Nor have they learned that this creative potential is awaiting recognition from them.

You have the opportunity to express your creativity staring you in the face every minute. If you haven't begun to express it, do so today.

—Bob Proctor

Remember to be creative in every area of your venture. It makes the game more fun and more productive.

In addition to creativity, patience is essential. Everything takes time, and things often do not happen overnight. Though you may suddenly find yourself with a "steal of a deal" property, unless you have cash on hand, the financing and closing process may stall or just not go as smoothly as you would like. It will take some time to develop a team that works as a team, and it will take time to develope a real-estate portfolio and reputation where you are taken seriously as an investor. Stay focused on your intended outcome. When problems or stressful situations arise, take a deep breath, step back from the plate, and loosen up. Look for solutions outside the box. Use creativity and ingenuity to solve the dilemmas that arise. Brainstorm daily. Look for new ways to accomplish the tasks before you, but most importantly, have fun while doing it. If the task becomes too stressful, your passion for the game will dwindle, and you'll lose your edge. Remain fit mentally and physically and always be willing to walk away from a deal. If it's not working out, there may be good reason, and there will not be a lack of investment properties or buyers for that matter, even in today's market decline. Remember, even Babe Ruth struck out often. But with practice, determination, and a winning team, you do have the potential to swing and make your real-estate investments your own shot heard 'round the world.

Chapter Nine

Postgame Activities

Landlording: Do It Yourself or Professional Property Management

You have acquired the perfect property; now it is time to define your rental strategy. Do you manage the property yourself, or do you hire a professional property manager? You should perform some of what I'm about to discuss during your investigation of the property. It's ideal to know, or at least have a pretty good idea about, your target tenants and the amount of rent that can be charged.

If the subject property is located more than an hour's drive away, you may consider hiring a property manager, unless purchasing and managing rentals is your full-time occupation. In either case, you should be familiar with the process of finding and managing tenants.

The buy-and-hold strategy provides you with three income streams. The first is amortization where the mortgage gets paid (ideally by the rent[s] collected) and the amount owed decreases. Next, the property increases in value while you own it, or appreciates. The final income possibilities are the tax advantages you gain as a landlord and business owner. Many of your investment and operating costs are deductible. Make sure you consult your tax team member about deductible expenses.

It is very important that you get a copy of the state Landlord Tenant Act. Study it carefully and have a thorough understanding of all rules and how you are affected by them. If you are not sure, consult your real-estate attorney about all of your rights as a landlord.

The amount of the lease should be based on a market analysis of other properties in the area, the number of rentals available, how your rental compares with others, and what prospective tenants will pay for your advantages, such as a garage, fireplace, extra room, pool, or other amenities. What are the rental terms, for example, due date, lease period, pets, guests, property uses, who pays cost (utilities, garbage removal, etc.), late fees, carry-over fees, and deposits? There is a lot to consider, so before taking this on yourself, working with a professional property manager may save you time, money, and irritation.

If the property is located within a homeowners association, make sure their rules allow rentals. You should pay the monthly dues and include them in the rent. You do not have to break this out—simply factor it in the base rent. This is for your protection; as the owner, you should always pay anything that may cause you to lose the property or have a lien placed on it. If the tenant is fined for breaking the rules, you pay the fine and charge it back to the tenant. Be sure this is spelled out in the lease and that the tenant gets a copy of the rules of the homeowners association.

Remember, security deposits are the tenant's money and should be held in a separate account until the tenants vacate.

You should set up an operating account for this particular property. This is the account where you put the rents and pay for repairs and taxes. You should build a reserve in this account for unexpected or emergency repairs and regular maintenance. Be aware that most states have specific laws regarding emergency repairs to maintain the property in a livable condition. Be sure you know the law, because if problems are not fixed, the tenant can move to suitable temporary housing *at your expense.*

You also may need the reserve for times between tenants when the property is vacant; for cleaning, repairs, and painting; and for advertising for new tenants. It should be noted that repairs required to keep the property in working order are your responsibility, as well as emergency repairs. Tenant damage, damage by visitors and family, and damage by lack of common sense are the tenant's responsibility.

The next major step is finding a tenant. You can advertise for tenants in several ways: newspaper and Internet sites (some, such as craigslist.com, are free), PennySaver ads, flyers, yard signs, real-estate offices, and sometime the most effective, word of mouth. Residents of the neighborhood can be a good source because they can choose their neighbors.

Screening tenants is a big part of this process, and it is best if you develop a standard screening process. Do the same thing over and over. All tenants must be treated the same (fair housing law). You can save a lot of time and money by screening out bad tenants, but it takes practice to identify the signs of a bad tenant. This is the most critical part of finding tenants. There are several standard points of concern when screening tenants: rental, financial, criminal, and work histories.

The tenant application should have all of the following information: names (applicant and coapplicant) of all who will be living in the residence (including children and in-laws), current address, phone numbers, Social Security number(s), occupation, employer information (salary and contact information), other sources of income, pets (type and weight), references (personal and professional), vehicle information (year, make, model), bank information, prior residences (landlord with contact information and reason for moving out), current debts (car payments, alimony, and credit card balances), bankruptcy (when and why), smoker or not, crimes, and prior evictions or delinquencies. Last, the application must include an authorization for you to investigate the information provided. It should contain language similar to the following: "I declare that the information and statements above are true and correct. I hereby authorize verification of all information given and the obtaining of consumer credit reports, criminal record(s), rental history, employment records, police reports, and any other reports deemed necessary by the landlord and at any time deemed necessary by the landlord."

Rental history includes items like were rent payments late or offered with excuses, were they considered good tenants, did they provide notice prior to leaving, was the property in good shape, and if not, what was the damage, did they have animals, and what was the length of tenancy? Call at least two former landlords for references. Ask if there were any problems. Ask why the prospective tenant left. Ask for their rental history and any issues that occurred.

Financial history includes questions like do they pay debts and how, are they using credit and how much, have they had a bankruptcy, and are they applying for a lot of credit? You should always run your own credit checks. You will need the tenant's permission to run a credit check, so get a signed authorization. You can check with national tenant networks to receive a complete tenant screening, including rental, credit, criminal, and personal checks. Contact credit bureaus. Be aware of the Fair Credit Reporting Act when screening prospective tenants. The laws are very specific governing credit checks, and violations need to be fully understood.

Criminal history factors include: How long ago did any offenses occur and what were they: drugs, crimes against children, crimes of intimidation, identities theft, armed robbery, or assault? Check with local police departments.

When investigating work history, how long has the applicant been at their current job or at least with the same company? How many jobs has he or she had in the past? Do they have growing income? What are the reasons for leaving their last job? Check with the employer, and ask about wages, length of employment, and last evaluation rating. Are there attendance problems?

There are many good sources for advice in this process. An article by attorney Janet Portman posted on www.nolo.com entitled "Choosing Tenants: Avoid Fair Housing Complaints and Lawsuits" reminds the reader to not only check the typical background information listed above but to also "make decisions based on business reasons." Leave your personal attachments or judgments out of the decision. Have a standard by which you approve applicants and stick to it. You will find that friends and family will ask you for favors to rent to a family member or person in need. While this may be OK, understand that these tenants will be expected to live up to the terms of their lease. Always take a lease even for family members. It protects you and them as well.

As with any business, it may be fine to donate or make some charitable donations through your business as these may be tax deductible, but you cannot give your products and services away. If a friend or relative is not well suited as a tenant or you feel cannot properly maintain the residence, reconsider doing any favors. This is your business. Treat it as such. Again, make sound business decisions while treating people with respect.

You can do it yourself; there are abundant resources available to screen tenants. Make a commitment to read real-estate-related articles and books at least weekly. We all know that we sometimes need reminders of how to do things more efficiently and effectively. Even the best athletes have coaches. Decide how you want to proceed, and do it the same way every time—yet be willing to improve your batting average and fitness!

Landlord Tenant Act

As a landlord, you have to know the laws and legal issues regarding renters. This might require a new lineup. Remember to use your team members wisely and capitalize on their specific skills and talents in this part of the game, too. Investors should seek legal advice to understand the state laws where the property is located. State laws vary; however, they all apply to residential properties, including single-family residences, multifamily residences, and apartments. The Landlord Tenant Act deals with fair housing.

The basic concepts are to protect the public from discrimination due to race, color, religion, natural origin, handicap, and familial status (children). Your attorney or realtor may become your batting coach here until you comfortably play a few innings.

Under the Landlord Tenant Act, the landlord and tenant obligations and remedies for landlord noncompliance and penalties are defined. Tenants can be difficult, but evicting or refusing to maintain the property just because they irritated you may earn you a hefty fine. Though professional ballplayers may seem to react to fines with nonchalance, remember that fines and disregard for the law, even if you are unaware of the law, may mar your business reputation and disrupt your cash flow to the point of insolvency. Use your team members to help coach you through this process. Each state's laws vary, and you should study them for the states in which your rental properties are located. You can stay abreast of the statutes and compare difference by visiting Websites such as http://realestate.findlaw.com/tenant/tenant-resources. Consider using professionals until you can navigate these pages and spot changes and differences comfortably.

The following stipulations are from Arizona's Landlord Tenant Act: the failure to return security deposit is remedied with the landlord returning two times the deposit, plus the original deposit. Failure to deliver has a remedy of a voidable lease.

"Self-help for minor defects" could end up costing you a bundle, and not just in dollars. Simply put, this is when the tenant makes repairs on his or her own, and the remedy is half of a month's rent to pay for repair. With self-help issues, the landlord always has to be notified. Most of the time, the problem occurs after the tenant has lived in the home for some time. They also have to produce receipts for stated repairs. These are repairs that the landlord is responsible for, according to the lease. For example, a tenant might fix a minor leak in the roof that is technically the landlord's responsibility. A broken window is also a good example, but who broke the window?

If the tenant's children broke the window, they would not be able to deduct the rent. If it was broken upon move-in or it was broken by high winds blowing debris, the landlord is responsible. Most of the time, the landlord will make repairs to avoid this. This law is in place to protect the tenant from the landlords who refuse to repair minor items. No one wants to be a slumlord. Providing quality housing in good repair is the ethical way to do business.

Allowing property to fall into disrepair is a bad business practice and can lead to more serious issues, such as a failure to supply essential service for health. An example is a malfunctioning sewer system or lack of a heating system in some climates. This is remedied by the tenant moving into temporary housing at the landlord's expense, although the tenant must still pay rent. In the case of repairable fire and casualty damage, the situation is the same as essential services: the landlord pays to move the tenant into temporary housing while they continue to pay rent, or lease is voidable. In the case of eviction due to construction issues, the renter can also move to another location until the work is done or the lease is voided.

Under Arizona's Landlord Tenant Act, the remedy for noncompliance by tenant's failure to pay is a court proceeding for eviction. Five days notice is required to inform the tenant prior to requesting a court date. A court date *to schedule eviction* is required, and the costs for this step are the tenant's responsibility, as are costs for forcible entry and detainer court request of eviction to retake property. A writ of restitution eviction order (may include owed monies), sheriff's removal of tenant (eviction), and a distrait provision, which allows the landlord to take personal property to get repayment of tenant's debt, can all be charged to the tenant.

In Arizona, if a tenant is absent from the property and all personal property is gone with rent unpaid, a ten-day rent notice has to be posted. If the tenant is gone for ten days without notice and the rent is not paid, a 30-day rent notice must be posted in plain view. In Arizona, this is considered abandonment. Violation of the Landlord Tenant Act carries a maximum of $10,000 fine. This can sorely affect future seasons. It is imperative that you are clear on the various state laws if you have properties in multiple states. In such a case, be sure to have at least one team member there who will keep you abreast of the law.

There are several necessary documents in addition to the tenant application required to lease your property: the lease contract with specific addendums (insurance, pet, and swimming pool); notice of eviction; notice of overdue rent; lease termination agreement; payment agreements; and move-in/move-out checklist. You should also be aware of the local laws regarding excise taxes.

Addendums call attention to and tie tenants to rules to protect you. Only use addendums for very specific items of concern. All other terms and conditions should be in the lease. The lease must document expectations, define lease terms and length, establish rent and deposits, define parties to the lease, define the property, and provide contact information for all parties to the lease. Sample leases are available on the Internet, in office supply stores, and sometimes in locally owned establishments that also offer mail services, and in good stationery stores. However, it is advisable to talk with your attorney when you first get up to bat for this inning. When I first started with residential properties, I used my attorney to write the leases. She was my pinch hitter until I got enough practice. After the first few, I used her leases as a guideline and drafted my own from that point on. I would have her review the lease only if I had a specific concern with a tenant or a particular property.

A notice of eviction is the landlord's notice to the tenant that they are being asked to leave the premise and remove all possessions *unless certain conditions are met* within a prescribed time period. It should also describe the actions that will immediately be pursued if the conditions are not met. Typically, this is the eviction process prescribed by state law, and standardized copies of the process may be available at office supply houses or via your attorney or realtor. As in the case of tenant screening, take the same action every time.

A notice of overdue rent is the landlord's notice to the tenant that the rent has not been received. It should reference property address, have the time period for which the rent is past due, the amount due, the late charge on the outstanding balance as provided in the lease, and should cite the lease terms verbatim. The late charge can be a flat fee or a percentage of rent per day overdue. Most important, it instructs where to send the payment. Your first objective is to get the rent, and it helps to make it as easy as possible to defend your position should additional action be necessary. Of course, all documentation of nonpayment should be kept in duplicate or triplicate because you may need these to support the eviction process should that become necessary. Whenever you mail documents or notices to the tenant, always send them certified with a return receipt. This is your proof of notification to the tenant, even if the tenant refused the mail or does not pick it up at the post office.

A lease termination agreement is a notice that the lease is about to expire. You should send this notice at least 30 days before the termination of the lease. This notice should state the termination date and time as described in the lease, it should stipulate that the tenant's possessions will be removed from the premises (leased property), and it gives complete possession to the landlord at that time. Lastly, it should state the actions that will be taken by the landlord should the tenant not vacate the premises. Many landlords will offer an existing tenant a new lease, but this is not necessary if you are unhappy with the tenant and feel you can replace them quickly or without disruption to your cash flow. But trying to show a property that is still occupied by a tenant who is being asked to leave at the end of a lease may cause some discomfort. Consider lease renewal only after examining the tenant's payment history and the condition of the property.

You may choose to use a payment agreement. If a tenant is behind on the rent or having a problem paying the rent due to an unforeseen circumstance, the tenant can sign a payment agreement stating the time period by which he will pay the amount owed in full. Consider the excuse, including timeliness—did the tenant let the rent fall behind before informing you, or did they notify you prior to the due date? How likely is it that they can catch up? It is likely many of their bills have fallen behind if they cannot meet their housing costs. But there might be extenuating circumstances, and good tenants can sometimes hit a foul ball or make an error. A payment agreement is a good faith exercise on your part that states that if the terms of the payment agreement are not met, the tenant agrees to vacate the premises and give the landlord permission to change the locks and remove the tenant's personal belongings and place them on the street. The tenant also agrees to pick up his belongings within 48 hours after the locks have been changed, though you are not responsible for items left outside on the curb or simply outside the residence.

A move-in package should contain a signed copy of the lease, address labels for mailing rent or other correspondence to the landlord, a copy of direct deposit instructions (if you use this), a copy of the intent to vacate letter for when they want to move out, a receipt for security deposit and other deposits (pet, cleaning, etc.), emergency numbers, insurance addendum, lead-based paint disclosure (if the home is older than 1978), and any other disclosures that are necessary. Note: be sure your receipt for funds specifies what amount is security deposit and what amount is not (refundable verses nonrefundable). Also, if the funds are noncertified, make sure the check is good and clears prior to move in.

A move-in/move-out checklist is a two-part form. You complete the first part, with pictures of the residence, and the tenant completes the second part during the walk-through inspection prior to taking possession. You can provide the tenant with a move-in form when they receive the keys, which they can mail to you within a specified period of time. It is wise to have the lease state that the move-in form is due within ten days of the receipt of the keys or the tenant will be responsible for condition of the premises upon move-out. At move-out time, you fill out the same form and compare the two. The tenant should have the opportunity to be at the move-out inspection.

The move-in/move-out form should contain a list of every room in the residence, including garage, exterior walls, and landscaping. There should be space next to each room's listing for comments. If an item is not applicable, then it can be left blank or N/A can be written there. Each item should have a comment next to it (such as "good," "needs repair," "not working," etc.). The items on your list include walls/ceiling, floors, trim, windows, screens, window coverings, light fixtures, sink, and toilet. Other items include tub/shower, medicine cabinet, exhaust fan, towel rack, cabinets, range/oven, refrigerator, dishwasher, garbage disposal, washer/dryer, heater, air conditioner, evaporative cooler, exterior walls, exterior trim, fence, gates, garage door openers (how many) and any other items that may be specific to your property.

Rent is simply the amount of money owed to the landlord every month. Depending on the jurisdiction, an excise tax may or may not be due. This is the tax charged by governmental bodies for the right to rent. You could consider it property tax for the renter. The landlord collects it and passes it to the government whenever rent is collected. This should be specified in the lease. Rent raises should be specified in the lease and usually occur on the anniversary (renewal) of the lease. Normally, you should give a 30-day notice prior to increasing the rent. Large rent increases may force tenants out. Remember, most of the time, an occupied rental is better that a vacant one.

When thing are going well, the rent is received on time with good funds. However, when things are not going well, what are your options? The first option is charging late fees. Late fee amounts vary from state to state, but generally they are 1 percent of the rent per day and are retroactive to the rent-due date. Usually, a letter to the tenant must be postmarked the day the rent was due, and the tenant has a three-day grace period to make payments before late fees can be assessed.

If the tenant still has not paid the rent or negotiated a payment agreement, your other option is eviction. Remember, if you accept partial rent, you lose your right to evict the tenant. Under normal circumstances, a landlord should only accept full rent. In order to avoid losing your right to evict, you must have a written agreement with the tenant that can be a wavier of rights, a payment agreement, or right of eviction agreement. Team members can instruct you on what written agreements are necessary in accordance with your state or local laws. This is yet another reason to have professionals on the roster.

There are several other reasons for eviction besides nonpayment of rent. Some examples for eviction include falsification of documents, illegal discharge of a weapon, criminal behavior including prostitution, threatening or intimidating behavior, infliction or threat of serious bodily harm, unlawful manufacture, selling, storing, keeping, or giving of a controlled substance, failure to meet conditions of lease, or not maintaining the premises. In these instances, you will need proof in the form of before and after pictures, police reports, or notices sent to tenants explaining the violation with a time frame for the tenant to correct the violation. The process for these evictions is the same as for nonpayment of rent (see section about Tenant Landlord Act). Before you decide to handle evictions on your own, be sure to consult your team members and educate yourself. A great article for getting the feel for this type of situation is "How Evictions Work: Rules for Landlords and Property Managers" from Findlaw.com. It will give basic steps for the process, but again, this should be part of your education and not to be entered into without professional advice until you are comfortable with the law and the proceedings. Simply changing the locks isn't going work. In fact, it may begin a very nasty battle.

Your lease should state that you reserve the right to inspect the property with a 24-hour notice. Maintaining a good, professional, yet friendly relationship with tenants may help prevent things from getting out of control. Don't let problems escalate in hopes that your tenant will know what you expect.

When a tenant moves out you have (according to Arizona Revised Statutes) 14 days to provide an accounting of the security deposit. Other states allow 30 days. This general accounting should show amount of deposit, itemized list of tenant's responsibility, items charged against the security deposit, and the amount returned to tenant. Some items that might be charged to the tenant include cleaning of appliances, carpets, and baths, et cetera; repairs to premises (e.g., walls, ceilings, and floors); landscape repair/ maintenance; and junk removal. A good practice at move-in is to provide the tenant with a list of average costs that could be charged upon move-out.

The Internet is an abundant source for information on all topics, but it can be difficult to know which online sources are good and which are bogus. So here are some tips for your new business venture. They are a good starting point for research. As you become affiliated with professional organizations and other professionals, you'll not only be directed to their Websites and articles, you may find it helpful to write your own. Writing books, articles, and blogging helps increase your visibility and credibility in the real-estate world and in business in general. Keep a journal of your own as you gain experience. For example, an article titled "Top Ten Tax Deductions for Landlords" (www.montcopropertymanagers.com) gives simple, pragmatic advice on deducting, interest, depreciation, repairs, local and long distance travel, home-office expenses, employee and contractor services, expenses, casualty and theft losses, insurance, and legal and professional services. The piece is written by attorney and author Stephen Fishman. By mentioning legal and professional services last, the article leaves the reader feeling the necessity for *seeking* legal and professional advice. But such articles are great sources of information on organizing your finances, remaining abreast of what to save for your accountant, and/or dealing with tax advisors. Exposure for your own business can be furthered in this same way.

Property Management

Choosing the right management is crucial, but so are your relationships with managers and tenants. Having the right team is number one, but being the team player is just as important. Understanding your role is vital. Tyrants are often not successful landlords. Learning to leave the ego out of property management, yet insisting on ethical standards from both management and tenants, is an exercise in personal growth and maturity. The next section will encourage team dynamics, learning from crisis situations, and encourage the reader to learn from mistakes and move forward in his or her financial fitness.

A property manager manages and handles tenants and maintenance-and-repair issues for your rental properties. Your property manager is your eyes and ears. She should be able to handle eviction proceedings, inspections (inside and out) of the property, rent vacant properties for you, provide monthly income/expense reports, collect rents and late payments, and handle repairs and inspections. When owning out-of-state properties, it is best to hire a property management firm. Your property manager should have a 24-hour contact service and a backup in case she is not available. The manager handles security deposits, rents, and other charges; you are responsible for paying your mortgage, taxes, and homeowners association (HOA) dues. As with all the other services you bring onto your team, you need to know how property managers prefer to get paid.

A tenant-placement agent (which can be the property management firm) finds and places tenants. Your agent collects the security deposit. You should review and approve all tenant applications. Your agent should check references and run a credit report, then supply this information along with the lease for your approval. There should be no additional charges for showing property. Most tenant-placement agents work on a flat-fee basis, which is usually between 5 and 10 percent of the monthly rent.

The type of tenants desired is a very important issue for both your desires and *understanding*. Some fair-housing laws are federal laws and apply to the entire United States; you should familiarize yourself with them. However, states' laws differ. You need very clear legal advice on choosing tenants without violating fair-housing laws. Be sure you know the laws and that the manager or management company is following them. It is wise to have your legal advisor look over the standard leases issued by these companies and also to approve any clauses or addendums you may wish to add. For example, if you own a house in a neighborhood with a HOA, you will need to require that your tenants be held to the terms stated by the HOA bylaws. This might include lawn care, auto repairs done on the property, and other aesthetic issues. Ensuring this is worded correctly in the lease and that such issues are communicated effectively to the tenant can prevent fines from the HOA, which would be levied against the owner, not the occupant.

Commercial Leases: A Fan in Business?

Imagine that you own or manage a small business selling licensed sports apparel at sporting events and you want to lease a new building. You call the leasing broker listed on the sign out front. The agent meets you at the property, and you love it. You want to lease it right then to move in next week.

The agent informs you that the 4,500-square-foot building leases for $20 per square foot, or $90,000 for a one-year lease, arriving at a monthly lease price (with a one-year lease) of $7,500 per month. When you're ready to commit, he then tells you, "We have to agree on a lease price and terms first." Dumbfounded, you stare blankly back at him. Didn't he just tell the terms of the lease? It seemed simple enough.

"We need to fill out a proposal to lease," you are informed, and this is where your education really begins.

You meet the next day in his office, and he brings up the proposal to lease form for your review. You have no trouble establishing who the landlord is and the size of the space, but when he asks you what the name of your company is and who will guarantee the lease, you get a little nervous.

Your company, 1951 Giants Fans, LLC, has never registered its name with the secretary of state, and now he is asking you as the president to put your name on the lease and guarantee it. Well, it's all part of being in business, which is new to you, so you move on. Then he asks for the intended use. You say to sell licensed sports apparel. The broker says, "Are you going to make or print any of the merchandise here and sell it out of the front door? If so, we want to define the retail sales, manufacture, and main office operations as part of your use."

You also want to sublease some of the space to your accountant, CPA, and college buddy Mel, so you will want to include this use in the clause. All occupants or businesses operated from this location will need to be identified.

Next, you fill out the lease term and commencement sections. You expect a two-year commitment, and the broker tells you that a five-year lease is the minimum the landlord will allow and that he wants you to move in within 60 days! Your head is spinning; you think to yourself, "How do I know how big my company will grow in five years? And then they want me to move in right now!"

The rent issues he discusses next should be easy, but you find out to your horror that the $7,500 rent is just for starters. The landlord wants an annual rent increase of 5 percent a year, and when the taxes and utilities go up, he wants you to pay that, as well as the property management expense. Now you are really worried and pull out your cell phone. "Am I allowed to place a call to my friend Matt the attorney [another fraternity brother and possible joint tenant who is just getting his start in the legal profession and wanting to capitalize on your business connections]?" The broker says yes, but he suggests that you wait until the end of the proposal so that you will have a list of all of your questions.

At the end of this section, he mentions that he will need your credit report and that you will need to pay first and last months' rent, as well as a security deposit, up front. Your recent cash flow shortages make the sweat drip down your forehead and your heart race.

Next he asks you about any tenant improvements you might want. You were pretty happy with the space, but it needed a couple of new offices, painting, carpeting, and category five cabling throughout. "No problem," he says, "I think the owner will be willing to pay for half of it."

You sit up straight in your chair and think, "Why only half?" Then he mentions a tenant improvement allowance of $30 per foot. You realize you may have to use cubicles instead of walls because your aunt Clara really needs to be kept separate from your mother or they'll gossip and chat about family affairs all day long.

Then he explains that you are responsible for all of the maintenance inside the building during the lease term, including the doors, windows, and air conditioning, and that the owner will take care of the roof, exterior painting, asphalt, and sidewalks, and he casually mentions how generous this is for a commercial landlord but that it is because the building is new construction. He also points out the minimum level of insurance the landlord needs you to carry and that you need to pay for all of the utilities. In addition to phone, cable, and electricity, you will be responsible for water, sewer, gas, and garbage, and he retains the right to use your dumpster should need arise. Huh? How is that even right?

"Parking is another issue," he explains. "We have 25 spaces allocated for the building." The broker continues, "Signage is only allowed on the front of the building and is limited by city ordinance to 48 square feet. If you want to renew your lease, we should discuss the rates and time frames now. If you want to expand or contract in the future, we should also address this in the lease proposal."

With all of these expenses swimming in your head, you think that maybe you should own the building. He says, "Well, we could either include a right of first refusal to purchase the property or a right of first offer." By this time, you are so confused that you agree and hope the process gets over soon.

He prints out the proposal and asks you to sign and give him a first month's rent check to show that you are really serious about making this deal. You know that you don't have the money in your account, so you tell him that you want to review the draft of the proposal with your attorney and CPA and will get back to him. He looks disappointed, of course, because 10 percent of this is quite a monthly sum for brokering this deal. But he prints it out, and you leave with your hand on the cell phone, dialing Matt's number for legal advice. Money is the least of your worries.

You go back to your office and start working the numbers. Your current rent is half of the new rent, and with all of the additional factors and increases in mind, you realize that this particular space is too expensive for the time being. You call the broker and let him know you are going to pass, but then he mentions that the landlord is motivated and could give you three months free if you agreed to the lease. He had not mentioned this before, and it makes you stop and think.

But the time is not right, and you tell him you need a smaller, less expensive space. He smiles over the phone and tells you of another location that might just work for your budget. You listen to him, look at the property, and fill out another proposal that makes more sense to you and four months later are moved in.

The bottom line is that the lease proposal will make or break the deal. When considering commercial space, you need to plan ahead—years ahead—to avoid costly surprises and be certain you're comfortable with all the deal points. This is important no matter which position you are in, whether you're at bat or in the field. As a commercial landlord, the lease proposal is crucial, and it is imperative you have a qualified manager for the property because commercial leases are so different from residential leases.

Game Day!

A cold chill has blown over the real-estate market, and sales are down across the country. When the market was hot, every Tom, Dick, and Harry wanted to sell real estate. Why? Because hot markets do not take any skill, premier quality customer service, or talent. Now that the housing market has been on a steady decline, we have an opportunity to separate the good from the bad and the ugly.

There are actually agents who expanded their market share, added more clients to their portfolios, or received higher customer service acknowledgments during the last year. These are the agents who understand that in a down market, true real-estate professionals actually can do better.

Since it is no secret that the real-estate market is in crisis, there are strategies that will help keep existing investors operating with profits and may actually put them ahead of the game when the market returns. And it will. It always does.

Making the Most of Technology and the Internet

Make a daily search of new properties part of your routine. Time is of the essence, and being in the right place when new opportunities come online is crucial. Good deals are often bought up quickly. Sellers of all types, real-estate and other sales, often try their luck simply listing online. Google, Yahoo, or other search engines can help you navigate the abundant Websites where someone may list or even just be considering listing a property. Craigslist is a good site to find new listings. Simultaneously, your other activities, including marketing, MLS, and customer management, need to be integrated into one easily accessible, web-based system. Exposure online is crucial. Be sure to have your listings include words that are often used in keyword searches. Good webmasters or Website designers will be able to design your site so that people searching out specifics on properties will get hits on your site. This is another team member to have on reserve. Agents should be doing these things *now* to make sure that when the market turns, they will be able to process the entire property buying and selling transaction online. Virtual transactions have arrived.

Innovative web-based initiatives are emerging quickly, encouraging agents and other real-estate professionals to explore these services and see what new technologies and features may be added to strengthen their online portfolio and its exposure.

Effective Team Building

The concept of smaller more efficient teams of businesses within larger companies has been around for awhile, but during the last decade, the concept has gained momentum. "RE/MAX now estimates that 27 percent of their affiliates work on a team," according to the Swamponel Report published by Realsure. Basically there are two different kinds of teams. The first is where two or more producing agents combine their practices to provide more exposure and services for themselves and their clients. An agent who starts building a business inside the brokerage operation is another type of real-estate team. This agent then hires other staff such as receptionists, administrative and bookkeeping personnel, and property managers in order to increase his or her time available specifically for the scouting out of listing properties and selling them.

Forming your own team, whether large or small, is vital to building a successful business. Finding members whose chemistry is complementary to others on your staff and who can take and follow through with instructions or take action when needed is a great asset. Though you need to micromanage, you should also trust each person to do the job you've hired them to do. Be clear on your business plan, expect it to be followed, and play ball!

A Solid Business Plan

Competition in today's volatile market is fierce. Success is not guaranteed. Moving into a new year or a new opportunity without a well- and thoroughly constructed business plan can be disastrous. Yet so many investors are just winging it. They go up to bat without practicing for the current day's game.

A business plan must include:

- An assessment of your current situation, including capital on hand and cash flow or revenues coming in steadily
- A definition of your mission statement
- A clear vision of what results you want to achieve and how you intend to do so
- An understanding of why you need regular analysis and occasional revisions of your game plan, including scouting out new talent

Capitalizing on Internet Sources

The ways in which virtual assistants (VAs) can help real-estate agents become more productive are limited only by one's imagination. These individuals can handle paperwork, scheduling, client contact, and even book travel. You have all the benefits of an in-office assistant without the overhead. Albert Einstein said, "Imagination is more important than knowledge. For knowledge is limited to all we now know and understand, while imagination embraces the entire world, and all there ever will be to know and understand." Get creative with what you can do online. Once you get comfortable, you can use some online sources for accomplishing or delegating tasks. And there are few, if any, support functions that cannot be handled by a VA, including:

- Screen email and phone messages
- Staying in touch
- Ad writing
- Transaction coordination
- Listing marketing coordination
- Online lead management
- Operational management
- Website maintenance

Diversification

Diversification is the key to any successful investor. In real estate, there are two types of diversification: geographic and product or service. In these slow times, it may be wise to view your customer base to see if there are other profitable products you can offer. It is also a perfect time for agents to expand their skills by getting educated on other transactional aspects, such as mortgage, escrow, homeowner's insurance, home warranty, remodeling, repairing, painting, and landscaping. The advantage of bringing some of these services in-house is the ability to eliminate the expense of overhead by using some of your team members for a variety of tasks and services and to earn additional income from the same client. Your existing clients are a great source of additional revenue. Develop customer loyalty!

The Law of Attraction Help

While the Law of Attraction is quite popular these days, the concept has been around for centuries and has been known (and used successfully) by great minds throughout history. According to Rhonda Byrne's book *The Secret,* there's evidence that the Law of Attraction was used by Beethoven, Einstein, and even Jesus—but you've also used it in your own life whether you're aware of it or not! This is because the Law of Attraction works whether or not you're aware of it. The main reason for the current focus is that if you're aware that you're using the Law of Attraction, you can control what you attract into your life. You can use this concept to help smooth the buying and selling process, including having properties find you. And if you are a sports enthusiast, you're probably aware that successful teams always rehearse the game in their minds, imagining winning the game, the trophy, or the pennant!

How the Law of Attraction Works

You create your own reality. The explanation of this principle is that simple. What you focus on, what you think about, is what you draw into your life. What you believe will happen in your life is what does happen. Though the concept is simple, it seems that everyone would have the lives that they want naturally. But the problem is, people will momentarily focus on their desires and then flip their thoughts to fears of not getting it or not having it, or they focus on what they don't want. For example, many people focus on their debts with the intention to eliminate them, but when they look continually at the problem, it brings more problems.

Let's look at this in the real-estate business. Many people enter into contracts fearing that the deal will fall through, so problems arise and hinder the progress. We've all heard about people who suffer through the financing process and complain that "they keep requesting the same documents." The next time you have a simple business transaction, play with this idea. Focus on a smooth process with no additional hassles and a closing that occurs as scheduled, with all parties happy. It seems that many people take some convincing, but there may be a more pragmatic reason for it. When we're thinking positively, we can handle the minor details without letting them frustrate us.

Why It Works

Though there are numerous teachers, books, videos, CDs, and celebrities supporting this concept, including Oprah Winfrey, there are two main schools of thought that explain why the Law of Attraction works. There is the spiritual explanation and the scientific explanation. Depending on your personality and way of thinking, playing with the Law of Attraction and seeing it work in your life can be great fun. The spiritual aspects of it need not conflict with your religious or spiritual beliefs, nor should the scientific explanation be too far out for your education, even if your background is in the sciences.

The Spiritual Explanation

Many people believe that the Law of Attraction works by aligning God or the Universe with our wishes. In other words, your prayers assume God wants to reward us. The positive ones are working with the Law of Attraction to produce benevolent blessings, while the negative, fear-based prayers bring negative results. Think about this if you pray or meditate. What are you saying or asking for? Reword it if necessary. We are all made of energy. Essentially, this is what most religions and spiritual teachers refer to as "spirit" or the "soul." When we examine energy in a scientific perspective, we see that energy operates at different frequencies, or vibrations. This is true for our own energy. Everyone knows what you mean if you say something or someone has "bad vibes."

We can change our frequency of energy, or our vibes, with positive thoughts, especially gratitude for what we already have. By using these thoughts and feelings and by focusing on our dreams rather than our frustrations or irritations, we can change the frequency of our own energy, and the Law of Attraction can bring positive things to us. What we attract depends on where and how we focus our attention, but we must believe that it's already ours, or soon will be.

The Scientific Explanation

If you're one who needs things to be easier to prove, there is a different explanation for how the Law of Attraction works. By focusing on attaining a new reality, or changing our current financial and personal situations and circumstances, and by believing it is possible, we tend to take more risks, notice more opportunities, and open ourselves up to new possibilities. Also, when we *don't believe* that something is within the realm of possibility, we tend to let opportunities pass by unnoticed. We even say, "If something seems too good to be true, it probably is." There are those times when the "steal of a deal" is a reality. We can find that the right money, whether financing or the down payment, does come through unexpectedly. When we believe we don't deserve good things, we behave in ways that sabotage our chances at happiness. By changing our self-talk and feelings about life, we reverse the negative patterns in our lives and create more positive, productive, and healthy ones. One good thing leads to another, and the direction of a life can shift from a downward spiral to an ascent. And again, when we're living a happier and more positive life, the little things that arise, and eventually the big ones, do not have the same irritating and upsetting affect on us. We roll with it.

Research on optimism and positive thinking shows that optimists typically enjoy better health, greater happiness, and more success in life. Optimists focus their thoughts on their successes and mentally minimize their failures. And millions of people have found success with positive affirmations. Affirmations are statements we write and repeat to ourselves to replace the negative thoughts. Many people write affirmations on three-by-five cards or on small pieces of paper that they then tape to a place they see daily, such as the bathroom mirror or the computer monitor. You can write whatever you like, but it is suggested that you keep them in present tense, positive, and from an "attitude of gratitude."

You might want to start each affirmation with the phrase "I am so happy and grateful now that …

> *"I have $X in rental properties …"*
>
> *"I weigh X lbs."*
>
> *"I have $X in residual income from investments."*

Get creative and make them personal. You might even find pictures of specific properties, or ones that resemble the ones you'd like to own, and keep them in your line of vision throughout the day. Include some that seem easy to achieve ("I now own the four-plex on Elm Street") and those that seem nearly impossible. As you achieve the easier ones, you'll find you're a step closer to owning, buying, or selling larger properties, creating larger amounts of cash, and having a larger business portfolio than you imagined. By rehearsing these ideas continuously and seeing how they help in achieving your personal and business goals, one day you'll find your swing produces a home run … your own shot heard 'round the world.

Suggested Reading

"1031 Tax Deferred Exchange—5 Steps to Success," Jeanette Fisher

Arizona Residential Seller Advisory

"Avoid Traps in Government Leases," *National Real Estate Investor*

Bob Proctor, *Insight of the Day*

Real Estate Dictionary

John W. Reilly, *The Language of Real Estate*

Helpful Websites & Online Articles

"Silence Is Not Golden," Traci Ellis

thePepper.com

"Real Estate Investing Contracts on Toilet Paper," Dr. Phil Speer

"Top Ten Tax Deductions for Landlords," Stephen Fishman

burnsidewriterscollective.com

creatingstrategies.com

EzineArticles.com

"Finding Good Deals in Real Estate," Dan Auito

foreclosure.com

icle.org/newlawyers

Mortgagenewsdaily.com

Glossary

Adjustable-rate loans, also known as variable-rate loans, usually offer a lower initial interest rate than fixed-rate loans. The interest rate fluctuates over the life of the loan, based on market conditions, but the loan agreement generally sets maximum and minimum rates. When interest rates rise, generally so do your loan payments; and when interest rates fall, your monthly payments may be lowered.

Annual percentage rate (APR) is the cost of credit expressed as a yearly rate. The APR includes the interest rate, points, broker fees, and certain other credit charges the borrower is required to pay.

Conventional loans are mortgage loans other than those insured or guaranteed by a government agency such as the FHA (Federal Housing Administration), the VA (Veterans Affairs), or the Rural Development Services (formerly know as Farmers Home Administration, or FmHA).

Escrow is the holding of money or documents by a neutral third party prior to closing. It can also be an account held by the lender (or servicer) into which a homeowner pays money for taxes and insurance.

Fixed-rate loans generally have repayment terms of 15, 20, or 30 years. Both the interest rate and the monthly payments (for principal and interest) stay the same during the life of the loan.

The **interest rate** is the cost of borrowing money, expressed as a percentage rate. Interest rates can change because of market conditions.

Loan origination fees are fees charged by the lender for processing the loan and are often expressed as a percentage of the loan amount.

Lock-in refers to a written agreement guaranteeing a home buyer a specific interest rate on a home loan, provided that the loan is closed within a certain period of time, such as 60 or 90 days. Often the agreement also specifies the number of points to be paid at closing.

A **mortgage** is a document signed by a borrower when a home loan is made that gives the lender a right to take possession of the property if the borrower fails to pay off the loan.

Overages are the difference between the lowest available price and any higher price that the home buyer agrees to pay for the loan. Loan officers and brokers are often allowed to keep some or all of this difference as extra compensation.

Points are fees paid to the lender for the loan. One point equals 1 percent of the loan amount. Points are usually paid in cash at closing. In some cases, the money needed to pay points can be borrowed, but doing so will increase the loan amount and the total costs.

Private mortgage insurance (PMI) protects the lender against a loss if a borrower defaults on the loan. It is usually required for loans in which the down payment is less than 20 percent of the sales price or, in a refinancing, when the amount financed is greater than 80 percent of the appraised value.

Thrift institution is a general term for savings banks and savings and loan associations.

Transaction, settlement, or closing costs may include application fees; title examination, abstract of title, title insurance, and property survey fees; fees for preparing deeds, mortgages, and settlement documents; attorneys' fees; recording fees; and notary, appraisal, and credit report fees. Under the Real Estate Settlement Procedures Act, the borrower receives a good faith estimate of closing costs at the time of application or within three days of application. The good faith estimate lists each expected cost either as an amount or a range.

Goal Setting Worksheet

Specific

Measureable

Attainable

Relevant

Time-based

Real Estate Goals

1. ______________________________

2. ______________________________

3. ______________________________

4. ______________________________

5. ______________________________

6. ______________________________

Personal Goals

1. ____

2. ____

3. ____

4. ____

5. ____

6. ____

7. ____

8. ____

Mortgage Shopping Worksheet

	Lender 1	Lender 2
Name of Lender:		
Name of Contact:		
Date of Contact:		
Mortgage Amount:		

	mortgage 1	mortgage 2	mortgage 1	mortgage 2
Basic Information on the Loans Type of mortgage: fixed-rate, adjustable-rate, conventional, FHA, other? If adjustable, see below.				
Minimum down payment required				
Loan term (length of loan)				
Contract interest rate				
Annual percentage rate (APR)				
Points (may be called loan discount points)				
Monthly private mortgage insurance (PMI) premiums				

How long must you keep PMI?				
Estimated monthly escrow for taxes and hazard insurance				
Estimated monthly payment (principal, interest, taxes, insurance, PMI)				
Fees Different institutions may have different names for some fees and may charge different fees. We have listed some typical fees you may see on loan documents.				
Application fee or Loan processing fee				
Origination fee or Underwriting fee				
Lender fee or Funding fee				
Appraisal fee				
Attorney fees				
Document preparation and recording fees				
Broker fees (may be quoted as points, origination fees, or interest rate add-on)				
Credit report fee				
Other fees				

Other Costs at Closing/ Settlement Title search/Title insurance For lender				
For you				
Estimated prepaid amounts for interest, taxes, hazard insurance, payments to escrow				
State and local taxes, stamp taxes, transfer taxes				
Flood determination				
Prepaid private mortgage insurance (PMI)				
Surveys and home inspections				
Total Fees and Other Closing/ Settlement Cost Estimates				

	Lender 1	**Lender 2**
Name of Lender:		

	mortgage 1	mortgage 2	mortgage 1	mortgage 2
Other Questions and Considerations about the Loan Are any of the fees or costs waivable?				
Prepayment penalties Is there a prepayment penalty?				
If so, how much is it?				

How long does the penalty period last? (For example, three years? Five years?)				
Are extra principal payments allowed?				
Lock-ins Is the lock-in agreement in writing?				
Is there a fee to lock in?				
When does the lock-in occur—at application, approval, or another time?				
How long will the lock-in last?				
If the rate drops before closing, can you lock in at a lower rate?				
If the loan is an adjustable rate mortgage: What is the initial rate?				
What is the maximum the rate could be next year?				
What are the rate and payment caps each year and over the life of the loan?				
What is the frequency of rate change and of any changes to the monthly payment?				
What is the index that the lender will use?				
What margin will the lender add to the index?				

Credit life insurance Does the monthly amount quoted to you include a charge for credit life insurance?				
If so, does the lender require credit life insurance as a condition of the loan?				
How much does the credit life insurance cost?				
How much lower would your monthly payment be without the credit life insurance?				
If the lender does not require credit life insurance, and you still want to buy it, what rates can you get from other insurance providers?				

This information was prepared by the following agencies:

Board of Governors of the Federal Reserve System

Department of Housing and Urban Development

Department of Justice

Department of the Treasury

Federal Deposit Insurance Corporation

Federal Housing Finance Board

Federal Trade Commission

National Credit Union Administration

Office of Federal Housing Enterprise Oversight

Office of the Comptroller of the Currency

Office of Thrift Supervision

These agencies (except the Department of the Treasury) enforce compliance with laws that prohibit discrimination in lending. If you feel that you have been discriminated against in the home-financing process, you may want to contact one of the agencies listed above about your rights under these laws.

Closing Checklist

(Commonly Used Documents—Some Documents Will Vary from State to State)

Seller:

Buyer:

Property:

Lender:

Title insurance company:

Broker(s):

Closing date:

1. Warranty deed
2. Seller's closing statement
3. Buyer's closing statement
4. Commitment for title insurance
    a. Review easements, building and use restrictions, and other recorded instruments

   b. Confirm that all title insurance company requirements have been satisfied

   c. Mark-up at closing

5. Survey

6. Escrow agreements

   a. Occupancy

   b. Water

7. Estoppel certificate (regarding borrowed funds)

8. Owner's affidavit (regarding title matters)

9. Property Transfer Affidavit

10. Homestead Exemption Affidavit

11. Request to Rescind/Withdraw Homestead Exemption

12. Notice to Assessor of Transfer of the Right to Make a Division of Land

13. IRS Form 1099-S

14. Certification for No Information Recording (1099-S) on the Sale or Exchange of a Principal Residence. Use when gain on sale does not exceed $250,000/$500,000.

15. Bill of sale

16. Nonforeign person affidavit

17. Disbursement statement

18. Compliance agreement to correct documentation errors discovered after closing

19. 19. Standard one-year home warranty—often included when a broker sells a used home

20. Mortgage payoff letter

21. Loan documents for new mortgage loan

    a. Promissory note

    b. Mortgage

    c. HUD-1 settlement statement

    d. Federal truth-in-lending disclosures

    e. Waiver of escrow (if applicable)

    f. Uniform residential loan application

    g. IRS Form W-9, Request for Taxpayer Identification Number and Certification

h. Federal Emergency Management Agency standard flood hazard determination

i. Error and omissions/compliance agreement

j. Borrower's certification and authorization

k. Affidavit and agreement

l. Notice of assignment, sale, or transfer of servicing rights

m. Letter detailing monthly payment amount

22. Subdivision or condominium association status/payoff letter

23. Homeowner's policy of insurance

24. Cashier's check(s)

25. Keys, alarm codes, garage door openers, appliance warranties and manuals, etc.

26. Walk-through inspection to verify condition, repairs, etc.

27. Real-estate purchase agreement and amendments—review to determine closing documents and issues

This book is a home run, when it comes to real estate. As a real estate insider, Barnes gives some great tips.

—Gerry Robert, bestselling author of *Millionaire Mindset*

Becoming a master requires you to study your craft. Barnes has clearly mastered the ins and outs of real estate, and his book gives great advice.

—Bob Proctor, bestselling author of *You Were Born Rich*

Property is a great way to increase your assets. *The Property Game* breaks down the rules of the game, so that anyone can invest in real estate.

—Doug Meharg, building developer and
author of *Become a Richer You*

Barnes gives sound advice on real estate investing. It's a great starter book for anyone interested in the business.

—Dan Rodriguez, author of *Inner Secrets for the Everyday Landlord,*
founder of partnerforbusiness.com

About the Author

Graduating with a Masters degree in chemistry, William Barnes began his professional career in sales, field service and middle management for a Fortune 50 Company. In 1985, he left corporate America to start a software business, helping small to mid-size businesses become automated using PC computers. Barnes has also owned two manufacturer's representative firms and a manufacturing company.

In 1989, Barnes began a real estate investment career by purchasing, flipping and renting homes in Long Island. The experience taught him how to profitably purchase, hold and sell a place, as well as the ins-and-outs of being a residential landlord. In 1992, Barnes expanded to commercial real estate. In 2003, he moved to Arizona and became a licensed real estate agent and broker. Due to state laws, Barnes is entitled to write his own contracts in Arizona, whereas in New York an attorney is mandatory for contracts.

Barnes has been involved in more than 400 real estate transactions either as a buyer, seller or real estate agent. He attributes the majority of his fortune to real estate investments and advises others on how they can have the same successes.

Notes

Notes

Notes